This Bible belongs to

_____

It is a gift from

_____

_____

Bible Stories

for preschoolers

Text by
Monika Kustra

Adapted by
Betty Free Swanberg

Illustrated by
Andrzej Chalecki

Tyndale House Publishers, Inc.
Carol Stream, Illinois

Visit Tyndale's exciting website for kids at www.tyndale.com/kids.

TYNDALE is a registered trademark of Tyndale House Publishers, Inc.

The Tyndale Kids logo is a trademark of Tyndale House Publishers, Inc.

Bible Stories for Preschoolers

First English edition by Tyndale House Publishers, Inc., in 2011.

Originally published as *Opowiadania Biblijne dla Przedszkolaków* by Vocatio Publishers, LLC, copyright 2008, under ISBN 978-83-7492-034-6. Published by permission of Vocatio Publishers, Phoenix, Arizona, e-mail: ceo@vocatio.us.

English stories written by Betty Free Swanberg, based on original text by Monika Kustra.

Illustrated by Andrzej Chalecki

Designed by Daniel Farrell

Edited by Susan Taylor

For manufacturing information regarding this product, please call 1-800-323-9400.

Library of Congress Cataloging-in-Publication Data

Swanberg, Betty Free.
   Bible stories for preschoolers / text by Monika Kustra ; adapted by Betty Free Swanberg ; illustrated by Andrzej Chalecki. — 1st English ed.
      p. cm.
   ISBN 978-1-4143-3964-1 (hc)
   1. Bible stories, English. I. Chalecki, Andrzej, ill. II. Kustra, Monika. Opowiadania Biblijne dla Przedszkolaków. III. Title.
   BS551.3.S93 2011
   220.9′505—dc22
2011002959

Printed in China

17	16	15	14	13	12	11
7	6	5	4	3	2	1

Contents

THE NEW TESTAMENT

Dear Parents,

This dynamic book of Bible stories has been written and illustrated especially for your preschooler! You know how important it is to "direct your children onto the right path" (Proverbs 22:6), and this book is just the tool to help you accomplish that goal. As you read these stories and do the activities with your son or daughter, he or she will learn about key stories and people from the Bible. Along the way, children will discover more about God and his character, and about Jesus and how much he loves them!

Here are a few of the special features in this book:

* Engaging stories. The stories are at just the right level to keep a preschooler's attention.

* Colorful art. Every page is filled with colorful illustrations, giving your child an opportunity to "read" the pictures while listening to the stories.

* Family-focused activities. Following each story, you'll find questions to discuss and activities to do together with the whole family.

> *Talk:* Questions at the end of each story help your child comprehend the Bible account and apply it to his or her own life.

> *Do:* A simple activity reviews the message of the Bible story and engages your child in a hands-on way.

> *Remember:* Each story concludes with a Bible verse that relates to the lesson.

Enjoy *Bible Stories for Preschoolers* with your preschool child, and with your entire family!

Dear Boys and Girls,

Someone gave you this book of Bible stories. They gave it to you because they love you. They want you and your family to enjoy the Bible stories together.

You will hear stories about God and about people who learned to know him and love him. You will also hear lots of stories about God's Son, Jesus, and his Bible-time helpers, the disciples.

Take a look at some of the pictures in this Bible storybook. Do you see people you already know? If you don't know the people yet, that's okay. You'll be meeting a lot of new Bible-time friends!

Your family can enjoy the Bible stories in this book along with you. And you can all talk together about the stories. You'll even do some activities together and learn some Bible verses!

Are you ready? It's time to begin!

OLD
TESTAMENT

The World God Made

GENESIS 1:1–2:4

Close your eyes. Now, what do you see? You don't see anything, do you? Everything is dark.

That's how it was in the beginning. There were no flowers or trees. There was no sky where birds could fly. No lakes where fish could swim. No land where elephants and giraffes could run.

But God was there. And he was ready to make something!

In the beginning God made the heavens and the earth. At first there was only water. The water was everywhere. It was dark, and it had no shape.

God said, "Let there be light." And there was light! God saw that it was good. God called the light "day." He called the darkness "night."

That was the FIRST day.

The next day God said, "Let there be sky over the earth." And there was sky!

The sky was beautiful.

That was the SECOND day.

The next day
God said, "Let the
waters come together."
They did, and God called
it the "sea." God said,
"Let there be dry
ground." And there was
dry ground. God called it "land."

Then God said, "Let the land make flowers
and trees. Let it make fruits and vegetables." God
saw that all of it was good.

That was the THIRD day.

The next day God said, "Let there be lights in the sky." And there were lights! God created the sun to shine during the day. He made the moon and millions of stars to give some light during the night. And God saw that it was good.

That was the FOURTH day.

Do you know what God did next? He said, "Let there be fish to swim in the water." And there were fish! Then God said, "Let there be birds to fly in the sky." And there were birds! God saw that everything he had made was good.

That was the FIFTH day.

The next day was even more amazing. God said, "Let there be animals to walk on the land." And there were animals, big and small!

Finally God said, "I'm going to make someone very special. I'm going to create people who are like me." So God made people! He made a man. His name was Adam. Then God made a woman. Her name was Eve. God put them in charge of the fish and the birds and the animals.

God looked at everything he had made. He saw that it was very good.

That was the SIXTH day.

On the last day of the week, God rested.
He was done making things.

That was the SEVENTH day.

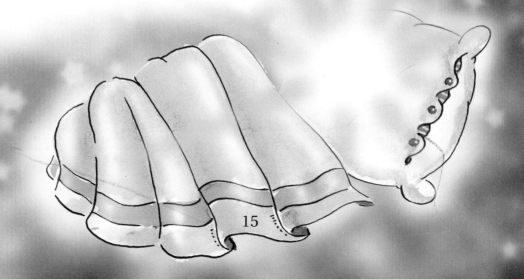

15

Family Time

Talk

* Talk together about how big God's world is and how perfect it was when God made it.

* Plan one way you can show thanks to God by helping to take care of his world.

* Say a thank-you prayer to God for something he made.

CREATION BOOKLET

Materials: seven sheets of paper, crayons, a family photograph, and tape or glue

Make a booklet titled "God Created the World." Number the sheets of paper. On each sheet, draw what God created that day and print the words "God saw that it was good." Tape or glue your family photo to the back of the last page. Take turns thanking God for creating each person in your family.

Remember

In the beginning God created the heavens and the earth.

GENESIS 1:1

Adam and Eve

GENESIS 2:8–3:23

Do you remember the name of the first
man God created? Was it Adam?
Yes, it was Adam!

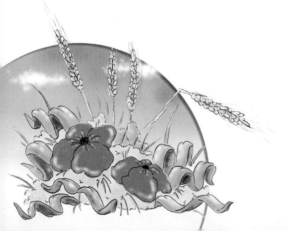

Adam needed a place to live. So God created a garden for him. It was called the Garden of Eden.

Many fruit trees grew in the Garden, and rivers flowed through it. There were beautiful birds and flowers and butterflies.

God was with Adam in the Garden. God cared for Adam the way a father cares for his children.

God brought the animals to Adam. Do you know how the animals got their names? God let Adam name them! Can you name some animals?

Adam liked the animals. But he needed someone like him to be his friend and helper.

God said, "It is not good for the man to be alone."

Do you remember the name of the first woman God created? Was it Eve? Yes, it was Eve! God brought Eve to Adam. The first man and the first woman were happy that they could live together in the beautiful Garden of Eden.

God told Adam that it was okay to eat any fruit from any tree except the one in the middle of the Garden. God said not to eat from the Tree of Knowing What Is Good and Bad. "If you eat fruit from that tree, you will die," God said.

One day an animal with a beautiful skin began talking to Eve. It was a snake. Can you find it hanging in the tree?

Eve didn't know who was talking. It didn't sound like Adam, and it didn't sound like God. Then Eve saw the snake. It was talking.

The snake asked Eve, "Is it true? Did God tell you and Adam not to eat any of the fruit in this Garden?"

"No, that's not true," said Eve. "We can eat most of the fruit. We just can't eat from the tree in the middle of the Garden. If we do, we will die."

"No, you won't die," said the snake. "Listen to me. Eat the fruit. Don't listen to God. He knows you will become wise like him if you eat the fruit. You will know what is good and what is bad."

Eve listened to the snake. She ate some fruit from the Tree of Knowing What Is Good and Bad. Then she gave Adam some fruit. He ate it too.

Right away, both Adam and Eve knew what was good and what was bad. But that didn't make them feel happy. It made them feel sad.

Do you know why Adam and Eve felt sad? They knew they had not obeyed God.

In the evening, Adam and Eve heard God walking in the Garden. They hid behind some bushes.

"Where are you?" God asked.

Adam said, "I'm hiding."

"Did you eat the fruit I told you not to eat?" asked God.

Adam said, "Eve gave it to me."

Eve said, "The snake told me it was okay to eat it."

God was angry with the snake. He said, "From now on, you will have to crawl in the dust."

God was upset with Adam and Eve, too.

It was wrong for them
to listen to the snake, who
was really God's enemy, Satan.

God said to Adam and Eve, "You
cannot live in the Garden of Eden
anymore." But God still loved Adam and
Eve. So he made clothes for them from animal
skins. And he cared about them even after he
sent them away from the Garden.

Many years later, God sent his own Son to earth. His name was Jesus, and he grew up to be more powerful than Satan. Jesus died on a cross and came back to life! Someday everyone who believes in Jesus will live in a place more beautiful than the Garden of Eden. It's called heaven, and God lives there!

Family Time

Talk

* What was the name of the Garden that God made for Adam and Eve?

* What did God say about the tree in the middle of the Garden?

* Talk about what happened because Eve listened to the snake.

* Name some ways God showed his love for Adam and Eve, and some ways he shows his love to all of us.

Do

GARDEN SHISH KEBABS

Ingredients: various fruits, whipped topping or melted chocolate, and skewers

Peel the fruit and cut it in small cubes. Put the fruit cubes on a skewer, one by one. Then pour melted chocolate on each fruit shish kebab or dip each one in whipped topping. Enjoy!

Remember

God made Adam first, and afterward he made Eve.

1 TIMOTHY 2:13

Noah

GENESIS 6:9–9:17

Noah loved God very much. So Noah obeyed God and made God happy. But there were many other people living on earth too. They did all kinds of bad things.

BUILD A BIG BOAT.

One day God said to Noah, "I see all the bad things that people do. I can't let them keep on acting that way. So I will send a big rain. The rain will fall for many days until water covers everything. But you and your family will be safe."

God told Noah just how to build a big boat. He told him to make it big enough for his family and two of all the animals, birds, and even crawly creatures!

Noah did what God told him to do. He began
to build a big boat. His three sons helped him.
But his neighbors laughed. They were thinking,
"The sun is shining. There is no water
anywhere. Where will Noah float
his boat?"

Noah knew that God would send rain. There would be a lot of water everywhere. So Noah kept working until the boat was ready.

Then the animals came—two of each kind. Big animals went into the boat. Small animals went into the boat. And all kinds of birds flew into the big boat.

Then Noah and his family went into the boat. Do you know who closed the door? God did! He wanted to be sure that Noah and his family and all the animals were safe inside.

Soon, small drops of rain began to fall. Then big raindrops came. Before long, it was raining so hard that the water covered the whole earth. But everyone in the boat was safe and dry.

After 40 days and 40 nights, the rain stopped. After five months, the boat landed on top of a mountain. But water still covered much of the earth.

Noah sent out a big, black bird, but it couldn't find a place to land. Do you see the black bird?

Then Noah sent out a white dove. Where is it?

At last the dove brought a leaf back to the boat. Then Noah knew that the water was almost gone.

After another week went by, Noah sent out
the dove again. This time it did not come back,
because it found dry ground.

When the time was right, God said to Noah, "Leave the boat. You and your wife may leave. Your sons and their wives may leave. All of the animals may leave. The birds may leave too."

The sun was shining when Noah and his family and the animals left the boat. They walked on dry ground.

Noah and his family praised God. And in the sky they saw something they had never seen before. Can you see it? Do you know what it is? It's a rainbow! God put it in the sky. He put it there to remind himself and everyone else that he will never cover the whole earth with water again.

Family Time

Talk

* Talk about what God told Noah to build.

* How many of each kind of animal went into the boat?

* Talk about how many days and nights it rained. How did two birds help Noah know when it was safe to leave the big boat?

* Who put the rainbow in the sky? What does the rainbow remind us that God will never do again?

OUR FAMILY BOAT

Materials: a large sheet of paper, a smaller sheet of paper, a pencil, crayons or watercolor paints, markers, glue, and scissors

Using crayons, markers, or paints, make a colorful rainbow on the large sheet of paper. Draw a boat on a small sheet of paper. Print your family members' names on the boat. Then cut it out and glue it under the rainbow.

Remember

[God said,] "I have placed my rainbow in the clouds."

GENESIS 9:13

Abraham and Sarah

GENESIS 12:1-9; 15:1-6; 17:1-8; 18:1-15; 21:1-7

Abraham was a rich man who worshiped God. But he lived in a country where other people didn't know God. So they didn't worship him.

One day God said to Abraham, "I want you to leave this country. I want you to move to a new country. I will show you where it is."

Abraham believed that God would show
him where to go, just as God had promised. So
Abraham and his wife, Sarah, put all their things
in big bundles. They put the bundles on top of
some of their camels.

Abraham took his whole family. He took all
his cows and sheep and donkeys, too.

Very slowly, Abraham
and his family and all his
animals began their trip
to a new country.

God was with Abraham and his family and his animals. God kept them safe as they traveled to places they had never seen before.

At last they came to the Jordan River. Do you see the river? They crossed the river and found themselves in a beautiful country. It was the land of Canaan. And it was the place where God wanted Abraham to live.

Abraham was glad to be in the new country. He prayed, "Thank you, God, for bringing my family and me to this place."

braham and Sarah lived in the new country
a long time. They had everything they
needed, and they were happy.

Many years went by, and every year Abraham
and Sarah each had another birthday. As they
grew older, they began to feel sad.

Do you know why Abraham and Sarah
were sad? They were sad because they had no
children.

God knew that Abraham was sad, so he told
him to go outside and look at the stars. God said,
"Abraham, you and your wife, Sarah, will have a
child. Then you will have grandchildren and great-
grandchildren. Someday there will be as many
people in your family as there are stars in the sky."
That's more than Abraham could count!

Abraham believed what God told him, and that made God happy. Many more years went by. But Abraham and Sarah still didn't have a baby.

Then God came to visit Abraham. He said, "Next year your wife, Sarah, will have a baby boy."

Sarah heard God. She laughed to herself and said, "Abraham and I are too old to have a baby."

God asked Abraham, "Do you think there is anything that is too hard for me? I am telling you what is true. Next year, Sarah WILL have a baby."

Abraham and Sarah had to wait another year for their baby. But they were glad that God did not forget about his promise.

What do you think happened a year later? Sarah had a baby boy, just as God had promised!

Abraham named the baby Isaac. The name means "he laughs." Baby Isaac laughed a lot. His parents laughed too. They were very happy. They knew that God had sent their baby to them at just the right time.

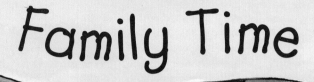

Family Time

Talk

* Talk together about God telling Abraham and Sarah to move. Has your family ever moved to a new place?

* Talk about the family God promised to Abraham. What did God ask Abraham to look at in the sky? Did Abraham believe that God would give him as many children as there were stars?

* Who did God send to Abraham and Sarah when they were old?

Remember

Ask and you will receive, and your joy will be complete.

JOHN 16:24

STAR CHAIN OF ANSWERED PRAYERS

Materials: a long piece of yarn, yellow paper, a pencil, scissors, a box, and tape

Cut out stars from yellow paper. Make them large enough so that you can print prayers on them. As your family prays together, print each prayer request on a star. Even if it takes a while, let the stars lie in a box until God answers. When he does, attach the star with the answered prayer to the yarn. You may want to hang the yarn across a bulletin board or on your refrigerator.

Jacob's Dream

GENESIS 25:19-34; 27:1–28:22

Do you remember baby Isaac? He grew up to be
a fine young man. After many years Isaac
became an old man. Do you see
him? He had two sons, Jacob
and Esau.

Jacob gave his brother,
Esau, a delicious meal,
but it was a trick.

Jacob tricked his brother into selling him a special family gift. Jacob tricked his father, Isaac, too. He did it by pretending to be Esau. Since Isaac could not see well, he gave Jacob the special family blessing. It was a blessing that belonged to Esau.

When Esau found out what Jacob had done, he was angry. Their mother was afraid that Esau might hurt Jacob. So she talked to Isaac, and they came up with a plan. She sent Jacob away. She sent him to his uncle's house, where he would be safe.

Jacob had to travel a long way to get to his uncle's house. At that time there were no trains or airplanes. There weren't any buses or cars. Jacob didn't even have a camel or a donkey to ride.

Jacob had to walk the whole way. When night came, he was tired.

Jacob had no bed. So he lay down on the ground. He didn't have a pillow, either. So he put his head on a hard stone.

Jacob heard strange noises. What do you think Jacob may have heard?

It was very dark. Do you think Jacob was afraid?

Finally, Jacob went to sleep.

While Jacob was sleeping, he had a dream. In his dream, he saw a long ladder. It reached all the way up to heaven. Do you know who was walking up and down the ladder? Angels! And God was at the top of the ladder.

God talked to Jacob. He said, "I am the God of your grandfather, Abraham. I am the God of your father, Isaac.

"I promised Abraham and Isaac that they would have many grandchildren and great-grandchildren. I am making the same promise to you, Jacob. You will have a very big family."

Then God said to Jacob, "I will give you a new home. I will go with you and be with you everywhere you go. I will protect you and keep you safe."

The next morning when Jacob woke up, he knew that God was with him. He said, "What an awesome place this is!" Then Jacob set up his stone pillow. He made it a special place to talk to God. And that's just what he did. Jacob was glad that God was there. He was glad that he could pray to God. He was very glad that God had promised to be with him.

Family Time

Talk

* Jacob had to leave home because he tricked two people. Who did he trick?

* Talk about the ladder and how God forgave Jacob and promised to go with him.

LADDER TO HEAVEN

Materials: wooden craft sticks, Popsicle sticks, or tongue depressors; glue; index cards; and a pencil

Make a ladder by gluing sticks together. On index cards, draw pictures or print the names of places you go (the store, church, a friend's house, the park). Stand the ladder on a desk or dresser, leaning it against a wall. Lay the cards around it and take turns picking up a card. Thank God for going with you to that place.

Remember

I am with you, and I will protect you wherever you go.

GENESIS 28:15

Joseph

GENESIS 37:1-28

Jacob went to his uncle's house. He worked hard. And God gave him a family that had 12 boys in it.

Jacob made friends again with the brother he had tricked long ago. Then he went home to his father. He stayed in the land where he grew up.

Jacob grew old. Do you see him? He loved all his children. But he showed special love for Joseph by giving him a beautiful long coat. Do you see Joseph's beautiful coat?

Joseph was happy. Look at the smile on his face.
But his big brothers were not happy.

The brothers became angry. They wouldn't
say one nice thing about Joseph.

Do you see two of the angry
brothers?

Joseph's brothers often worked in the fields. Sometimes Joseph did too. But his brothers didn't like him. Whenever one of the older brothers looked at Joseph, that brother looked like an angry cat.

The brothers tied wheat into bundles. Then they brought the wheat home. The wheat was ground up and used to make bread. Do you like wheat bread? Maybe you like to toast it.

One day Joseph told his brothers about a
dream he had. They were all tying wheat into
bundles. Joseph's bundle stood up straight.
But the bundles that his brothers
had tied together bowed down
to Joseph's bundle. Now the
brothers were really angry.
They asked Joseph,
"Do you think you
will be our king
someday?"

Soon Joseph told his brothers about another
dream. He told his father, too. "I dreamed that the
sun, the moon, and 11 stars bowed down to me."

Joseph's father, Jacob, wondered, "Will your
mother and I bow down to you?" Joseph's 11 big
brothers wondered if they were going to bow like
the 11 stars. Can you count the stars around Joseph?

Every day the brothers became more upset.

One day the brothers took their father's sheep to find grass to eat and water to drink. They didn't come back right away, so Jacob asked Joseph to go and find them. Jacob wanted to be sure that his older sons were okay.

Joseph walked for several days before he found his brothers. When they saw Joseph wearing his beautiful long coat, they said to each other, "Let's get rid of Joseph. Then we won't have to bow down to him. His dreams will not come true."

The older brothers were so angry that there was no love left in their hearts. So they made plans to do something very bad. They saw an old, dried-up well nearby. And they said, "We'll throw Joseph into that well. He won't be able to get out, so we'll just leave him there."

When Joseph came closer, his brothers grabbed him and took off his beautiful long coat. Then they threw him down into the empty well. Joseph couldn't get out.

The brothers sat down to eat. But soon they saw some men riding toward them. The men were traveling to the land of Egypt. There they would sell all the things they had with them.

The brothers sold Joseph to those men. The men gave the brothers a bag of money for Joseph. Do you see the bag? Now Joseph was a slave, and the traveling men could sell him to someone else in the land of Egypt.

Family Time

Talk

* Talk together about the special coat that Joseph's father gave him. How did that coat make Joseph's big brothers feel?

* Recall the dreams about the bundles of wheat and the sun, moon, and stars.

* Talk about how angry the brothers had become. Comment on how sad God is when we become angry and don't get along with our family or friends. Explain that God wants us to live in peace and get along with everyone.

COLORFUL COAT

Materials: crayons, paper, colorful fabric, scissors, and glue

Draw Joseph's face on the paper. Cut out a tunic (long coat) from the fabric and glue it to the paper under Joseph's head. Now draw his hands and legs. Talk about how family members can be happy for one another when they receive gifts. God is happy when families show love for one another.

Remember

Work at living in peace with everyone.

HEBREWS 12:14

Joseph in Egypt

GENESIS 37:31-36; 39:1–40:23

Jacob thought that his son Joseph was dead. He cried for a long time. Do you see Jacob's tears?

Jacob's older sons let him think that Joseph was dead. They didn't want him to know that they had sold him to some men who were going to Egypt.

By now Joseph was far away. He had come to the land of Egypt.

A rich man who worked for the ruler of Egypt bought Joseph. So Joseph had to work for this man. But he didn't get paid for the work he did, because he was the man's slave.

Joseph worked very hard. He lived in the rich man's house and did everything he was told to do.

God was with Joseph and took good care of him. God helped Joseph do his work well.

The rich man who had bought Joseph was very pleased with Joseph's work.

One day, the rich man said to Joseph, "I want you to be in charge of all the helpers in my house. Tell them what to do, and they will obey you."

So Joseph took charge of the helpers. God was with him, and everything in the house went well.

The rich man was happy, because he didn't have to worry about anything. The only thing he had to think about was what kind of food to eat!

But one day the rich man's wife told her husband a lie. She told him that Joseph had tried to do something very bad. She said that Joseph had tried to hurt her. Of course, that was not true. But the rich man didn't know that. He believed the lie his wife told him about Joseph. So the rich man became very angry.

The rich man wouldn't let Joseph work for him anymore. The man thought that Joseph would do something bad.

The rich man's wife knew that Joseph would not hurt her. She was the one who had tried to make Joseph do something bad. The wicked woman smiled a wicked smile. She had told a lie, so now Joseph would have to go to jail.

Joseph did not like having to stay in jail. He knew
that he had done nothing wrong. But Joseph also
knew that God was still with him.

The man in charge of the prison liked Joseph. So
he put Joseph in charge of all the other people who
were in jail. Joseph did his work well.

One man in the jail was a baker for Pharaoh, the king of Egypt. The baker had a strange dream. God helped Joseph know what the dream meant. Joseph said that the baker would die in THREE days.

Another man in jail with Joseph worked for the king by bringing him his food and drink. This man also had a dream. Joseph told him it meant he would get out of jail in THREE days. Then Joseph said, "Please ask the king to get ME out of jail too."

Everything came true as Joseph had said. But the man who got out of jail forgot about Joseph for a long time.

Family Time

Talk

* Why was Joseph's father so sad?

* Talk about how Joseph had to work for a rich man without getting paid. When the man's wife told a lie about Joseph, what happened?

* Point out that it was God who showed Joseph what the two men's dreams meant.

* Joseph still had to stay in jail because of the lie a woman had told about him. Talk about why we should tell the truth about others.

THE FAMILY PROMISE TO TELL THE TRUTH

Materials: a large sheet of paper, markers or crayons, and finger paints

Print on the paper, "We will always tell the truth because it makes God happy." Using the finger paints, place each person's handprint around the words to show everyone agrees with the promise. Hang up the family pledge. Be sure everyone knows the difference between telling the truth and telling a lie.

Remember

Stop telling lies. Let us tell our neighbors the truth.

EPHESIANS 4:25

Joseph, the Man in Charge

GENESIS 41:1–47:12

Many people have dreams. Even Pharaoh, the king of Egypt, had a dream. It was a very bad dream. He woke up in the middle of the night, and he was afraid. Does he look afraid in the picture? Do you ever feel that way?

Pharaoh sat up in bed. He remembered his dream. In his dream he saw some big, fat cows. There were seven of them. They came up out of a river and began eating grass.

Then seven skinny cows came up out of the river. They were very hungry. So they gobbled up the seven fat cows.

Pharaoh went back to sleep and had another dream. This time he saw seven fat plants growing in a field. They looked very healthy. He saw seven more plants in the field. They were dried-up and skinny. These plants gobbled up the fat ones.

The next day the king asked his wise helpers what the dreams meant. But they couldn't tell him.

Then the man who served the king his food and drink remembered Joseph, who was still in jail. "Joseph can tell you what your dreams mean," he said. So Pharaoh told someone to go get Joseph.

"Joseph," said the king, "I need your help. No one else can tell me what my dreams mean."

"I can't do it either," said Joseph. "But God can."

So Pharaoh told Joseph about his dreams. And God helped Joseph know what they meant.

Joseph said, "Both of your dreams mean the same thing.

"The big, fat cows and the fat, healthy plants mean that there will be seven good years in Egypt. Crops will grow in the fields, and there will be plenty of food to eat.

"But the skinny cows and the skinny plants mean that there will be seven bad years. Crops will not grow, and there will be no food."

Then Joseph told Pharaoh, "You must find someone who is wise. Put him in charge. He will have the people save some of the crops during the seven good years. Then there will be food to eat during the seven bad years."

Pharaoh said to Joseph, "You are wiser than anyone else. I will put you in charge." Then Pharaoh put his ring on Joseph's finger and gave him fine clothes to wear.

Now Joseph was a very important man in the land of Egypt. Only Pharaoh, the king, was more important than Joseph.

Everything happened the way Joseph said it would. During the seven good years, Joseph told workers to fill big buildings with crops from the fields.

Then seven bad years came. But the people of Egypt had food because Joseph had saved plenty of crops from the fields during the good years.

One day 10 men came from far away. They came to buy food. They were Joseph's brothers! How many can you see?

Joseph knew who the men were. But Joseph looked very different, so his brothers didn't know who he was. They bowed down to him and asked to buy food. Joseph told them to go back home and get their youngest brother. When they returned with his little brother, he told them who he was.

The older brothers were afraid. They knew they had been unkind to Joseph. So they thought Joseph might hurt them. But he didn't. He cried. And he said, "I am so glad to see you."

The brothers were sorry for being unkind. Joseph forgave them and sent them back to get his father, Jacob. Then the whole family came to live in Egypt, where there was plenty of food.

Family Time

Talk

* Talk about Pharaoh's dreams.

* Who told Pharaoh about Joseph? What did the man say Joseph could do?

* Recall who helped Joseph know what the king's dreams meant.

* Why did Joseph's brothers come to Egypt?

* Talk about how unkind the brothers had been to Joseph when they sold him. How did Joseph show that he forgave them?

SAVING FOOD AS JOSEPH DID

Materials: a glass jar; ingredients for granola, such as dry cereal, nuts, raisins, peanut butter, and honey; colorful fabric; scissors; glue; and ribbon

Make granola and fill a glass jar. From fabric, cut a rectangle as high as the jar and wide enough to go around it. Glue this to the jar. Put the lid on and tie a ribbon around it. Share the treat with one another, just as Joseph did when he forgave his brothers and shared some of the food he had saved.

Remember

You must forgive.

LUKE 17:4

Little Moses and Miriam

EXODUS 1:1–2:10

"Hush, my baby. Don't cry, my little boy." The mommy tried to keep her baby from making too much noise. The baby lived with his mommy and daddy; his sister, Miriam; and his brother, Aaron. Can you find each one in the picture?

The family with the baby boy lived in the land of Egypt. But they were not Egyptians. They were God's people. They were from the family of Jacob and Joseph, who had come to live in Egypt many, many years before.

A new pharaoh was the king of Egypt now. He didn't know God, and he didn't like God's people. He said, "There are too many of those people. I don't want there to be any more baby boys."

It was a sad time for God's people all over the land of Egypt.

Miriam wanted to help her baby brother. She wanted to do something good for him. She wished she could help keep her little brother safe.

One day Miriam's mother had a great idea. There was a river near their family's house. So Mother made a basket from a tall water plant. She covered the basket with tar so it would float like a little boat.

"We will hide our baby in his basket-boat. We will hide the boat in the water, near the tall grass."

Miriam was excited. Now it was her turn to do something good for her baby brother.

Miriam and her mother took the baby down to the river. They put him in his little basket-boat, and they placed the boat near the tall grass.

Miriam said, "I will stay and watch." So she stayed by the river, and Mother went home.

Miriam knew that God was with her. She knew that he would help her take good care of her baby brother. So she was happy to stay with him.

The baby felt safe in his basket-boat. He went to sleep as the basket rocked back and forth.

Miriam listened. She hoped that Pharaoh and his soldiers would not come. She didn't want them to find her little brother.

Pharaoh did not come. But Miriam kept listening and watching and praying.

Then Miriam heard some women talking together. Miriam hid in the tall grass by the river and watched to see what the women would do.

The women came closer to the river. One of them
was a princess. She was the daughter of Pharaoh,
the king!

The princess saw the basket-boat and wondered
what was in it.

Miriam watched as the princess looked into the
little boat and found the baby boy. Miriam didn't
know what to do. She was afraid. She wondered
what the princess would do with the baby. Was the
princess wicked like her father? Or was she a kind
person?

Miriam's little brother woke up and
saw the princess looking at him. He
began to cry. The princess felt sorry
for the baby boy. She was not wicked
like her father.

Miriam came out of her hiding place in
the tall grass. She went over to the princess
and asked her, "May I go and find a woman to
take care of the baby for you? I'll find one of God's
people."

"Oh, yes," said the princess. "Please do that.
Thank you."

So Miriam went to find her mother.

Miriam took her mother to the princess. The princess didn't know that this woman was the girl's mother and the baby's mother too. But the princess said to the woman, "Please take this baby home. I will pay you to take care of him."

Miriam helped her mother take care of the baby. He grew up to be a fine young man.

Then the princess let him live with her at the palace. The princess named him Moses.

Talk

* Talk about who was in baby Moses' family. Who is in your family?

* Recall why the baby boy's mother made a boat for him.

* Talk about the good things Miriam did for her little brother.

* What are some good things you could do for other people in your family?

* What did the princess do for Moses when he was older?

MOSES IN THE BASKET

Materials: a walnut, several colors of clay or Play-Doh, and a pencil

Split the walnut in half, and take the nutmeat out. Put some Play-Doh inside one shell for Moses' bedding. From pink or white Play-Doh, make a small ball for the baby's head, a cylinder for his body, and two small cylinders for his arms and hands. Place them in the shell, and use a pencil to make Moses' eyes and mouth. Then choose any color of Play-Doh for baby Moses' blanket.

Remember

Let's not get tired of doing what is good.

GALATIANS 6:9

Moses Meets God

EXODUS 2:11–4:31

Moses grew up in a palace in Egypt. He became a prince there. But he learned that he was really one of God's people. He looked around and saw that his people had to work hard for the wicked pharaoh. This made Moses angry. He knew it was not right for Pharaoh, the king, to be so unkind to God's people. So Moses tried to find a way to help.

Do you see the man carrying a load of heavy bricks? The work is too hard for him, but he is afraid to stop. He doesn't want to make Pharaoh angry.

Do you see two men trying to move one very big brick? They are doing their best, but it is hard for them to move the brick.

One day Pharaoh tried to hurt Moses. So Moses ran away from the land of Egypt.

After that, Moses was not a prince anymore. He became Moses the shepherd and took care of sheep. How many sheep do you see?

Moses took care of a whole flock of sheep. He helped them find grass to eat and water to drink.

Moses led the sheep to a mountain far away. He sat down and rested. But he watched the sheep while they ate. He wanted to be sure that they were safe.

While Moses sat by his sheep, he saw something that he didn't understand. He thought he saw a fire. Do you see the orange flames?

Moses wondered what was burning. He decided to go closer. So he got up and walked toward the fire. Maybe Moses thought he could put the fire out. Maybe he thought he could try to keep the grass and bushes from burning up.

When Moses came near the bush,
he thought to himself, "That's strange. The
bush keeps burning, but it's not burning up.
I've never seen anything like it!"

Then Moses heard a voice. It sounded as if it was
coming from the bush. "Moses! Moses!" said
the voice.

"I am right here," said Moses. "And
I hear you. But who are you?"

"I am God," said the voice from the
bush.

Moses got down on his knees and worshiped God. Then God said to Moses, "My people in the land of Egypt need help. I want you to go back there and talk to Pharaoh. Then lead my people out of Egypt. Take them to a new land."

"But what if the people won't follow me?" Moses asked.

"Tell them that I am God and that I sent you."

"But . . . but, I don't talk very well. My words get all mixed up."

"I will help you speak," said God. "I will tell you what to say. Your brother, Aaron, will help you too. Tell him what to say, and he will talk for you."

So Moses went back to Egypt. His brother talked to God's people for him, and the people listened.

* Talk about the wicked pharaoh and how hard he made God's people work.

* After Moses left Egypt, he took care of sheep. Do you remember what he saw one day while he sat near his sheep?

* Who talked to Moses from the burning bush? Talk about what God told Moses to do.

* What did Moses say he couldn't do? How did God promise to help Moses?

* What are some things that God helps you to do?

Do

MOSES' BUSH

Materials: an empty toilet-paper roll, orange and green construction paper, a pencil, scissors, and glue

To make flames of fire, let the youngest member of your family put his or her hand on the orange construction paper. Fingers should be spread apart. Trace around the hand, and cut it out. Print the verse below on the flames. Then stand the toilet-paper roll on one end and cover the roll with the flames. Cut out leaves from the green paper and glue them around the flames. Point out that the bush didn't burn up because God was in it, talking to Moses.

Remember

I will help you speak. I will tell you what to say.

EXODUS 4:12

Moses and Pharaoh

EXODUS 5:1–12:33

Moses and his brother, Aaron, were in Egypt, where God had told them to go. It was time to talk to Pharaoh. Do you see him? He is sitting on a throne. The back of it looks like a giant bird.

Pharaoh was an important man. He was the king who ruled over the land of Egypt. But he did not know God. And he did not like God's people.

Moses was not afraid, because he knew God was with him. And his brother was there too.

Moses told Pharaoh, "This is what God says: 'Let my people go out of Egypt so they can worship me.'"

Pharaoh said, "I do not know God. I will not let his people leave Egypt. They must stay here and work for me."

Then Pharaoh told his helpers to make God's people work harder than before.

So Pharaoh's helpers were unkind to God's people. The mean helpers made God's people get their own straw to make bricks. But they had to make just as many bricks as they did before.

God's people were upset with Moses and Aaron. They said, "Now Pharaoh has made more trouble for our people."

Moses and his brother went to Pharaoh again. But the king still wouldn't let God's people go out of Egypt.

So God made ten bad things happen to Pharaoh and the people of Egypt. God wanted them to understand how powerful he was.

The first bad thing that happened was that the water in all the rivers and wells got bloody. Do you see how red the water is? The fish couldn't live in the water. And the people couldn't drink it.

But Pharaoh wouldn't let God's people go.

The second bad thing that happened was that frogs were everywhere. God sent the frogs to the houses of all the people of Egypt. Most people like frogs when they see only one or two of them. But if they see hundreds of frogs, they get scared. Every time the Egyptian people turned around, they saw more frogs.

Pharaoh said to Moses, "I will let your people go. But ask your God to take the frogs away."

Moses prayed, and God took the frogs away.
But then Pharaoh changed his mind and would
not let God's people go.

So God made more bad things happen. The third
bad thing was that tiny flies came and bit the people
of Egypt. The fourth bad thing was that BIG flies
came, and they were EVERYWHERE!

Pharaoh kept promising to let God's people go.
But he broke each promise,
so God's people could not
leave the land of Egypt.

The fifth bad thing that happened was that all the animals belonging to the people of Egypt got sick. Before long, the Egyptians had no sheep or cows, because all their animals died. Only the animals belonging to God's people did not get sick and die.

The sixth bad thing that happened was that the people of Egypt began to get sick. They had sores all over their bodies. Only God's people were healthy. But Pharaoh still wouldn't let them go.

The seventh bad thing that happened to Pharaoh and his people was that big pieces of ice, called "hail," fell from the sky. The hail killed little plants, and it even killed big trees.

The eighth bad thing that happened was that big bugs called "locusts" came and ate all the plants that had not been killed by the hail.

But Pharaoh still wouldn't let God's people go.

The ninth bad thing that happened was that it was dark in Egypt for three days. It was like night all the time! It was so dark during the day that people couldn't see each other. But it was light during the day where God's people lived.

One day God said to Moses, "Get ready to leave Egypt. One more bad thing will happen, but you and the rest of my people will be safe."

God said that his people were to paint the top and the sides around the doors of their houses. They were to use the red blood from a lamb.

Then the tenth bad thing happened. The oldest son in every Egyptian family died. But God passed over the homes of his people and kept them safe. Finally Pharaoh said that God's people could go. And this time he really meant it.

Family Time

Talk

* Talk about why Pharaoh did not want God's people to leave Egypt.

* Look at the pictures to recall some of the bad things that happened to Pharaoh and his people.

* Talk about how God kept his people safe from the bad things that happened.

* Point out that God keeps us safe too.

THE FROGS

Materials: drawing paper, a pencil, scissors, and green crayons

Fold a sheet of drawing paper in half. With the fold at the top, draw a frog that looks something like the one at the bottom of page 106. Then cut the frog out, but don't cut around the top of its head. Use your cutout frog as a pattern to make more frogs. Color your frogs green, and send them hopping everywhere!

Remember

Don't be afraid, for I am with you. . . . I am your God.

ISAIAH 41:10

Moses in the Desert

**EXODUS 13:17–15:21; 17:1-7; 19:1–20:17;
31:18–34:4; 34:28**

Moses led all of God's people out of the land of
Egypt. Now they didn't have to work for wicked
Pharaoh anymore. They were free to move to the
land God had promised would belong to them
someday.

Moses didn't
know where to take
the people, but God showed him
where to go.

God went ahead of Moses and
the rest of the people. He sent a
big, white cloud to show the people
where to go during the day. God
sent a tall cloud of fire, too. The fire
showed the people where to go when
they traveled during the night.

Then Pharaoh and his army came
after God's people. He wanted to
take them back to Egypt! The people
were afraid, but Moses told them not
to be.

Moses and the people were near the Red Sea. God told Moses to hold his hand up high. When Moses did what God said, the wind blew part of the water to one side and part of it to the other side. In the middle was a dry path to walk on!

Moses went first, and God's people followed him. God kept them all safe.

God's people walked between the
water that was piled up high on each
side of them.

Pharaoh and his army were right
behind God's people. They started to cross
the Red Sea on the dry path too. God's people
hurried, and finally they came to the shore on
the other side of the sea.

When all of God's people were safe on the other side of the Red Sea, God told Moses to raise his hand again. Moses did what God said. And the water on each side of the dry path came back together. Then there was no dry path anymore.

Pharaoh and his army tried to go back to Egypt. But it was too late. The water covered them, and they couldn't get away. So God's people were safe. There was no one left to chase them.

Moses and his sister, Miriam, and all of God's people sang a thank-you song to God.

Then Moses and all of God's people began walking through the desert, where it was hot and dry. They got thirsty, but they ran out of water. The people were upset.

God told Moses, "Hit that rock over there. Water will come out of the rock, and the people can drink it." God took good care of his people.

One day God's people came to a high mountain
called Mount Sinai. The people waited while
Moses went up to the top of the mountain. God
talked to Moses up there.

"I have led you, and I have kept you safe,"
said God. "Now if you and the people will obey
me, you will be my own special treasure. You will
be more important to me and more loved than
anyone else."

Moses went down the mountain.
He told the people what God had said.

"We will obey God," the people said.

Moses went back up the mountain.
He talked to God again.

Several days later there was a lot of thunder
and lightning. And a big cloud came down on the
mountain. The people knew that God was there.

God had ten special rules for his people to follow.
God gave his rules, called the Ten Commandments,
to Moses.

The Ten Commandments help God's people know how to live and be happy. God said,

"I am your God. I am the only true God. You must not have any other god but me.

"You must not make any animal or human shapes from wood or stone or metal. Do not pray to any such object.

"Use my name only in kind and loving ways.

"Worship me on the seventh day of each week.

"Love and obey your father and mother.

"Do not kill anyone.

"If you marry, always be a loving and loyal husband or wife.

"Do not steal.

"Do not lie.

"Do not become upset and angry when you can't have everything that your neighbor has."

When
God finished
giving his
ten rules
to Moses,
God wrote
them on
two big stone
tablets.

Then Moses went
down the mountain with the
stones. But the people were busy.

Moses saw that while he was up on the
mountain, God's people had been doing something
they should not have done. They had taken some
gold and had made it into the shape of a
young cow—a calf. Do you see the gold
calf? The people were praying to the
gold animal. How sad! They should
have known that the calf couldn't
hear them. They should have
been praying to God.

124

Moses was angry when he saw the gold calf. He was upset because the people had disobeyed one of God's ten rules. It was the one that said not to make animal shapes or pray to them.

Moses broke the stone tablets on which God had written his rules. Moses told the people what a terrible thing they had done. He asked God to forgive them. God did. And he wrote his ten rules again. He wrote them on two new stone tablets.

Family Time

* Look at pages 114 and 115. Talk about how God led his people out of Egypt, giving them a cloud to follow during the day and a tall pillar of fire to follow during the night.

* On pages 116 and 117, find the walls of water. Only God could have made the path.

* When the people had no water to drink, what did God tell Moses to do to a rock?

* Reread the Ten Commandments on page 122, and talk about how obeying each one helps us to be happy.

* Let your child know how much God loves him or her. Explain that we show love for God by obeying his rules.

Talk

THE TEN COMMANDMENTS TRAIN

Materials: light-colored construction paper, scissors, glue or tape, and a pencil or marker

Draw a train engine and 10 cars on the construction paper (one or two cars per sheet). Print on the engine, "The Ten Commandments." On each car, print one commandment. Cut out the engine and cars, and connect them with glue or tape. Hang the train low on a playroom wall. Talk about how we are like treasures to God and about how he has given us rules to help us be happy. We show our love for God by obeying his rules.

Remember

If you will obey me . . . you will be my own special treasure.

EXODUS 19:5

Hannah's Child

1 SAMUEL 1:1-23

Hannah wanted to be a mother. But she and her husband had no children. That made Hannah feel very sad. Sometimes she cried.

"Why are you crying?" Hannah's husband asked. "And why won't you eat?"

Hannah's husband loved her. But he didn't understand that she needed a child to be happy. "Isn't it enough that you have me?" he asked.

No, it wasn't enough for Hannah to have a husband. She wanted a baby, too.

Another woman had several children. She made fun of Hannah and laughed at her. The other woman and her friends were unkind.

Every year Hannah and her husband went to a big worship tent. Many other people went there too—even the unkind woman and her friends.

At the worship tent, Hannah talked to God. Do you see her? She prayed, "Dear God, you know how sad I am. You know how much I want to have a child of my own. Please let me be a mother."

Hannah kept on praying. "Dear Lord, if you give me a son, I will let him work for you. When he starts growing up and gets bigger, I will let him come and live in this worship tent. I will let him do whatever you want him to do."

When Hannah prayed, she did not pray out loud. She moved her lips, but no one could hear what she was saying to God.

Eli was a priest who lived in the worship tent. Can you point to Eli? He wondered why he could not hear the words that Hannah was saying.

Eli thought Hannah's behavior was very strange. So he talked to her about it.

Hannah told Eli, the priest, how sad she was. She said she had been praying. She had been asking God for something special.

"Well, then," said Eli. "May God answer your prayer by giving you what you have asked for. Now go home and be at peace."

"Oh, thank you, sir," said Hannah. Now she didn't feel sad anymore!

Hannah began to eat again. The next day she and her husband and the other people went back home.

About a year later, Hannah had a baby boy.

Hannah named her son Samuel. She said, "I asked the Lord for him, and he answered my prayer." Hannah took good care of Samuel. Do you see him? Hannah kept her little boy with her while he was growing up.

Family Time

Talk

* Talk about why Hannah was sad.

* Discuss how unkind the other woman in the story was. Explain that adults as well as children should learn to be kind and show love for God and for others.

* Talk about Hannah's prayer and God's answer. Think about different ways God may answer our prayers, and why. (*No*, because it wouldn't be good for us. *Wait*, because we don't need it yet. *Yes*, because God wants us to have all the good things we need.)

* Talk about gifts God has given you.

PRAYER CLOUDS

Materials: dark blue and light blue or white construction paper, scissors, ribbon or yarn, hole punch, and markers or a pen

Cut out a large cloud from the dark blue construction paper to help you think about God. Now cut out some small clouds from light blue or white paper. Print on each one something you would like to ask God for. Punch a hole at the top of each prayer cloud. Then punch several holes near the bottom of the large cloud. Use ribbon or yarn to attach the small clouds to the large one. Point out that God hears all our prayers and gives us everything that is good for us.

Remember

**God cares about what we say.
God listens to us.**
1 JOHN 5:14-15

Samuel and Eli

1 SAMUEL 1:24–2:11; 3:1-21

Samuel was getting to be a big boy. So his mother, Hannah, knew it was time to take him to the big worship tent.

At the worship tent, Hannah saw
Eli. She asked Eli, the priest, "Do you
remember me? I was here several years
ago. You saw me when I was praying.
I asked God to give me a child. And he
did! Here is Samuel."

Then Hannah told Eli that she
wanted Samuel to be his helper. She
said, "Samuel will help you do God's
work."

Samuel was a happy helper. He did
his work well.

Samuel lived with Eli in the big worship tent. They both worked hard all day. One night they were very tired. Eli went to lie down in his big bed, and Samuel went to lie down in his little bed.

Samuel closed his eyes. All of a sudden, he heard his name. "Samuel!"

He wondered why Eli was calling him. The boy got up from his bed and ran to see what Eli needed. "Here I am. Did you call me?"

"No, I didn't call you," Eli said. "Go back to bed and get some sleep."

Do you see the lamp Samuel is holding? The fire gives him light so he can see in the dark worship tent.

SAMUEL!

When Samuel was back in his own little bed, he heard his name again. "Samuel!"

What do you think Samuel did? He got up and went to Eli again. "I'm here. Did you call me?"

"No, it wasn't me," said Eli. "Go back to bed."

Samuel didn't understand who could be calling him. Only he and Eli were in the tent.

Back in his bed, Samuel listened. And sure enough, he heard his name again. "Samuel!"

Once more Samuel got up and went to Eli. This time Eli knew that God was calling Samuel's name. So Eli told Samuel to say, "Speak, Lord. I am your servant, and I am listening."

So Samuel went back to bed. And he heard his name again. "Samuel! Samuel!"

This time Samuel said, "Speak, Lord.
I am your servant, and I am listening."
Samuel listened to God that night. And after
he grew up, he became very wise. Everyone knew
he always listened to God.

* Talk about why Hannah took Samuel to the big worship tent.

* What did Samuel hear one night?

* Act out the calling of Samuel. Let your child play Samuel, and speak Samuel's words with your child.

* Talk about who was calling Samuel's name that night.

* Discuss the fact that most of us don't hear God's voice, but we learn what he wants to teach us when we read and listen to Bible stories.

Talk

Family Time

Do

REMINDER SIGN FOR LISTENING TO GOD

Materials: cardboard or poster board for a sign, a marker, an unsharpened pencil, and tape

Print the verse below on your sign. For a handle, tape one end of a pencil near the bottom of the back of the sign at the middle. Before you read a Bible story or another verse, hold up the sign, and say this verse.

Remember

Speak, Lord. I am your servant, and I am listening.

1 SAMUEL 3:9

David the Shepherd

1 SAMUEL 17:34-35; PSALM 23

David took care of sheep, so he was called a shepherd. How many black sheep do you see? How many white sheep? David kept his sheep safe from snakes and wild animals.

Every morning, David got up early.
He took his father's sheep to a grassy place
so the sheep could eat the grass. David also
helped the sheep find water to drink.

David called to his sheep. Do you know what the
sheep said? "Baa! Baa!" The sheep knew David. They
knew that he was their shepherd and that they were
safe with him. So they followed him. And he used
his big stick to keep the big lions and bears away.
Do you see David's stick?

When the sheep were thirsty, David, their shepherd, led them to water. He took them to a quiet stream where the water was not deep. The sheep felt safe with their shepherd.

David often talked to God while watching the sheep. David thought to himself, "God watches over me just as I watch over my sheep. God is like a shepherd, and I'm like one of my sheep!" David felt happy as he watched his sheep and prayed. He got out his harp and began to play a song. He made up the words and the music. It was a beautiful song of praise to God.

   While David played his harp, he sang, "The Lord is my shepherd. I have everything I need. He helps me rest in the green grass. He leads me to quiet places where there is water to drink. He leads me along safe paths and makes me strong. Even when I walk through a dark valley, I will not be afraid, because you, God, will be close by.

   "I know for sure that God will always love me. And someday I will live with him forever!"

Family Time

Talk

* Talk about what a shepherd does.

* Why do you think sheep are happy to follow their shepherd?

* How did David use his stick?

* Talk about how God is like a shepherd and how we are like sheep. Thank God for being your Shepherd.

MUSIC FOR GOD

Materials: items to make musical instruments

You can make a drum from an oatmeal box and two sticks or unsharpened pencils. Use pot covers for cymbals. Make a horn from an empty paper-towel roll and waxed paper secured at one end with a rubber band. For maracas, put beans or pebbles in small jars. Now praise God with music as David did.

Remember

The LORD is my shepherd.

PSALM 23:1

David and Goliath
1 SAMUEL 16:1, 10-13; 17:1-50

David the shepherd was the youngest
boy in his family. God wanted David
to be king someday. But for now,
Saul was the king. And David's older
brothers were soldiers. They were soldiers
in King Saul's army.

One day David's father said to him, "Here is some bread and cheese for your brothers. I want you to take it to them." Then David's father said, "I want you to check on your brothers. See if they are okay. After you find them, come back home and tell me how they are."

So David left the sheep with another shepherd, and he began walking toward the camp where his brothers were. He went to see if they were safe or if there was fighting going on between them and their enemy soldiers.

David came to the camp. There he saw that his brothers and their friends were afraid. They didn't trust God to help them fight the wicked enemy soldiers. David talked to his brothers and their friends. They told him about Goliath, the giant.

Goliath was a soldier in the enemy army. He was so big that other men looked like little boys next to him. And he was mean. King Saul was looking for someone to fight wicked Goliath.

David's oldest brother was angry with him. "What are you doing here, David?" he asked. "You should be back home taking care of your little sheep. You don't belong here." But then King Saul heard that David was asking questions about Goliath. So the king sent for David. And soon David was talking to King Saul.

153

Do you see the wicked giant, Goliath? Do you see how afraid David's brothers are of Goliath?

David told King Saul, "Don't worry about anything. I will fight the wicked giant."

"You can't do that," said King Saul. "You are just a boy."

"But I take care of my father's sheep. When a lion or a bear tries to hurt one of the sheep, I fight the wild animal. And I win, because God helps me. I can fight the giant, Goliath, too. And I will win, because God will help me."

Goliath made a giant fist. He opened his giant mouth and yelled at King Saul's soldiers.

"Just send one man to fight me," said the wicked giant.

King Saul's soldiers were afraid to fight. So finally the king told the shepherd boy, David, that he could fight the giant, Goliath.

The king wanted David to wear a hard helmet to keep his head safe. He wanted David to wear armor made of heavy metal to keep his body safe. And the king wanted David to have a sharp sword. But David said, "I can't wear this helmet. I can't wear this armor. I can't use this sword."

So David wore his own clothes and didn't carry a sharp sword. But he did find five smooth little stones in a stream of cold water.

David put the five stones in a leather pouch called a sling. And he carried his shepherd's stick as he began walking across the valley. He was ready to fight Goliath.

Goliath saw David's stick and laughed. "Do you think I am a dog? Is that why you are coming after me with a stick?"

David said, "You only have a sword. But I have God with me."

Then David took out a stone and put it in his sling. He swung the sling around and around. Can you see David's sling? The stone hit the giant, Goliath, and knocked him over. He fell to the ground with a loud THUMP!

Now King Saul and his soldiers didn't have to worry about the wicked giant anymore.

Family Time

Talk

* Talk about what shepherds, kings, and soldiers do.

* Find the picture of Goliath shaking his fist. Talk about what makes him so scary and how you would feel if you saw him.

* Why did David believe he could win a fight with the giant, Goliath?

* Talk about how David won the fight. Point out that it was God who helped him know how to use the sling and the stone.

* What problems can God help *you* with?

DAVID'S STONES

Materials: five flat stones, a marker or watercolor paints and a paintbrush

Find five smooth, flat stones during a walk in your neighborhood. Print or paint one letter of David's name on each stone. The stones will remind you and your family that God helped David fight an enemy giant with a little stone. When we have a giant-sized problem and a little faith that God *will* help, God helps us, too.

Remember

Our help is from the LORD, who made heaven and earth.

PSALM 124:8

Saul and David

**1 SAMUEL 18:5-16; 19:8-10; 22:1-4; 27:1-4; 31:1-6;
2 SAMUEL 1:1-11; 2:1-7; 5:1-5; 22:1-4**

King Saul needed a leader for his soldiers. So he
asked David to be the leader. David was a good
leader, but the king soon became angry with him.

One day King Saul tried to hurt David. The king

was upset because he knew that David was a better leader than he was. He knew that all the people liked David. They sang and danced for David, but they didn't do that for Saul.

David was a good leader because he loved God and God was with him.

Saul was not a good leader. He did not love God, and God was not with him.

King Saul should have been glad that David won his fight with Goliath. The king should have been thankful that David was a good leader. But instead, King Saul was angry with David.

The king didn't like David, and that made David feel sad. He knew that he had to go away to a place where he would be safe from the king.

David moved to another country for a while. His parents and his brothers also moved there. Then David moved to a different place. He had to keep moving so that King Saul couldn't find him.

One day David learned that the king had died. King Saul had done a lot of bad things to David, but David still felt sad.

Then David became the next king. Do you see the happy people? Do you see the crown on David's head?

The shepherd boy David was now King David. Instead of caring for sheep, his new job as king was to care for all the people of the land. The people were happy to have David as their king.

It was God's plan for David to be king. Way back when David was a shepherd boy, he knew that God wanted him to be king someday. He just had to wait for the right time.

David sang a song of praise. He praised God for keeping his promise to him and making him king. "You kept me safe. Thank you, God!"

Family Time

* Talk about why King Saul was angry with David and tried to hurt him.

* What does the Bible story say about why David was a good leader and Saul was not a good leader?

* Talk about what David had to do so that he would be safe from Saul.

* When King Saul died, who became the new king?

* Talk about God's plans for David. Why did David praise God?

Talk

KING DAVID'S CROWN

Materials: construction paper, scissors, crayons, glue, and colorful tissue paper

To make a crown for King David, cut two wide strips of construction paper. On one edge of each strip, cut off a row of small triangles. Then glue the strips together to fit your head. You may decorate your crown with crayon circles and squares. You may also want to glue on balls of tissue paper.

Pretend to be King David, and read God's words in the verse below. Recall that God had good plans for David. What plans might he have for you?

Remember

I know the plans I have for you.

JEREMIAH 29:11

Elijah

1 KINGS 16:29-33; 17:1-16; 18:1-2, 17-46

Saul was the first king of Israel. David was the second king. Many years went by, and many kings ruled over Israel. Some of them, like David, loved God and obeyed him. Other kings, like Saul, did not love God or obey him.

Now Ahab was the king. He was a wicked king. He didn't believe in God. He and his wife, Jezebel, worshiped Baal, a fake god made of stone. Baal could not hear or answer their prayers.

Wicked King Ahab gave orders to have stone statues of Baal placed all over the land of Israel. Many people worshiped this fake god made of stone.

King Ahab and his wife, Queen Jezebel, were very wicked. They were more wicked than any other king and queen of Israel had ever been.

God was angry with King Ahab. God knew that it was Ahab who led many other people to worship Baal, the fake god. The people were not obeying God's rules. They forgot that God said, "You must have no other god but me. You must not make any animal or human shapes from wood or stone or metal. Do not pray to any of those things."

Some people did not forget about God and his rules. Elijah was one of those people. Elijah was a prophet who gave people messages from God.

Elijah told Ahab, "There is only one God. He told me that there will be no rain for several years. Not a single drop will fall on the land until I say it will."

Then God told Elijah to run quickly from the palace where Ahab lived. God knew that Ahab would be upset. So God told Elijah to run and hide by a brook, where he could get water to drink.

Do you see Elijah running to hide?

God sent some big, black birds to help Elijah. They were called "ravens." The ravens brought food to Elijah. They brought bread, and they brought meat. Can you find a black bird?

The birds brought food every morning and every evening. And Elijah drank water from the brook. But after a while the brook dried up. It dried up because there was no rain, just as Elijah had said. The plants and trees dried up too. The trees lost their leaves, and no crops grew in the fields. So the people had no grain to make food.

God knew that Elijah was hungry and thirsty. So God sent him to a little town to find food and water. God said, "A woman there will feed you."

When Elijah came to the little town, he saw a woman picking up sticks of wood. Elijah asked her for a drink of water and some bread.

The woman told Elijah that she had no bread. She was going to use the wood she had gathered to build a fire and cook some food. There would be just enough for herself and her son.

"Don't be afraid to make bread for me, too," Elijah said. "God told me that you will have enough flour and oil to make bread until it rains again. Then crops will grow, and there will be food."

So the woman cooked for Elijah, her son, and herself. She kept on cooking day after day. And every day there was enough flour and oil to make more bread.

God was taking care of Elijah. And he was taking care of the woman and her son just as he had promised.

After three years God said to Elijah, "Go to King Ahab and tell him I will send rain." Elijah didn't run away and hide this time. He went to see the wicked king. And the king came out to meet him. Do you see the king and his soldiers?

King Ahab said to Elijah, "You came back, did you? All you do is make trouble for everyone!"

"No," said Elijah. "It's you and your family who make trouble. You do not obey God. You worship Baal, who is a fake god made of stone. Baal is not the true God."

Then Elijah told King Ahab to have all
the people come to Mount Carmel.
"And bring your 450 prophets of
Baal," said Elijah. So that's
what Ahab did.

Elijah talked to the people. "You must choose who it is that you will worship. Will you worship the Lord God of heaven and earth? Or will you worship Baal, who is made of stone?"

Then Ahab built an altar where people could worship Baal. And Elijah built an altar where people could worship the true God.

Elijah said to the prophets of Baal, "Pray to Baal. If he is the true God, he will answer by setting the wood on the altar on fire."

The prophets of Baal prayed for a long time. They prayed louder and louder. But there was no answer. Baal did not set the wood on fire. Baal did not hear their prayers. Baal was not the true God.

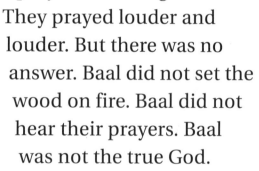

Now it was Elijah's turn to pray.
He poured water on the altar where
he would worship the true God.
It would be a miracle if fire burned
up water!

Elijah prayed, "O God, you made
heaven and earth. Hear my prayer.
Let the people know that you are the
only true God."

Right away, God sent fire. It
burned up everything on the altar,
even the water!

The people cried out, "The Lord
God is the true God!" And they
stopped worshiping Baal.

That evening Elijah prayed
for rain. And guess what?
God sent the rain!

Family Time

Talk

* Talk about what King Ahab and Queen Jezebel did that was so wicked.

* Talk about what Elijah told Ahab and about how God took care of Elijah afterward—first by a brook, and then at the home of a woman and her son.

* After three years Elijah went back to Ahab. Talk about the two altars and how God showed that he is the only true God.

* When Elijah prayed for rain, what did God do?

ELIJAH'S RAVEN

Materials: a paper lunch bag, a black crayon, pencil, yellow and black paper, scissors, and glue

Color the paper lunch bag black. Trace both hands of your youngest family member on a piece of black paper, and cut out the shapes for the raven's wings. Then draw a beak on the yellow paper and cut it out too. Glue all of the pieces to the black paper lunch bag. Draw the raven's eyes on the bag.

Remember

The LORD is God in heaven above and on the earth below. There is no other.

DEUTERONOMY 4:39

Daniel and His Friends

DANIEL 1:1-21

Daniel was a young man who lived in a big city. It was the city of Jerusalem. Many of the people who loved the one true God lived there.

Daniel and his friends went to school in the big city. They learned about letters and numbers. They learned to read and write and do number problems. They learned about God, too.

Three times every day the people in Jerusalem would pray. They would pray when they heard the sound of a horn. Do you see the horns in the picture? They are made from sheep horns.

The people prayed in the morning. They prayed at noon. And they prayed in the evening.

After the evening prayer, Daniel and his family would enjoy eating a good meal together. They always ate a lot of healthy food, like fruits and vegetables. They ate some good bread, too.

Daniel's father thanked God for the food he gave their family.

There was a high wall all around the city of
Jerusalem. It had been built many years ago.

The wall helped to keep God's people safe
because their enemies couldn't get inside. The
enemies would have to come through a gate,
which was like a huge door. Soldiers stood guard
by the gates day and night.

But one day the soldiers on top of the wall saw the king of Babylon. He was coming toward the city of Jerusalem. And he had his army with him. His soldiers were ready to fight the soldiers inside the big city.

After many days, the Babylonian army was able to break through the wall around the city.

The wicked king and his soldiers went into God's big, beautiful house. But they didn't go in there to worship God. They didn't even believe in God. So they didn't care that it was God's house. They just wanted some of the beautiful things inside. They stole many items made of gold.

Then the enemy king told his soldiers to take some of the young men of Jerusalem back with them to Babylon. He said, "I want strong, healthy young men. Make sure that they are good students. I want young men who have learned many things."

Daniel and his friends were strong, healthy, and smart. So they had to leave Jerusalem and travel through the desert to Babylon. It was a long trip.

When Daniel and his friends came to Babylon, the king put one of his helpers in charge of them. He said, "Teach these young men all about Babylon. And give them a lot of food from my kitchen."

Daniel and his friends liked to study. So they didn't worry about learning new things. But they did worry about eating the king's food. They knew that God didn't want them to do this.

So Daniel asked the king's helper to give him and his friends some vegetables to eat. The helper was afraid that the king would be upset with him. But Daniel said, "Let us try it for ten days."

After ten days, Daniel and his friends were stronger than the young men who ate the king's fancy food.

Every day Daniel and his friends ate vegetables
and drank water. And every day they learned new
things. They understood everything they read,
and they became very wise. They always knew
what to do.

Daniel learned what dreams meant. He learned
from God. And he talked to God every morning,
noon, and evening.

For several years, Daniel and his friends ate the good vegetables that helped to make them strong, healthy, and wise.

One day the king of Babylon talked with all the young men from Jerusalem. The king asked questions and listened to the answers the young men gave. He liked Daniel and his friends best of all. He could tell how strong, healthy, and wise they were. They understood everything.

The king asked Daniel and his friends to work for him. He knew that they were much smarter and wiser than anyone else in his whole kingdom.

Daniel worked for the king for a long time.

Family Time

Talk

* Talk about what Daniel learned at school as he was growing up.

* Talk about the city of Jerusalem and what happened to the wall around it.

* Where did enemy soldiers take Daniel and his friends?

* What did Daniel and his friends eat instead of the king's food?

* Why did the king of Babylon want Daniel and his friends to work for him?

LEARNING NEW THINGS

Materials: pictures from magazines and books that show things you are learning to do, this Bible storybook, and other books

Look at pictures, and identify things you are learning to do. (Get dressed, jump, skip, hop, listen to stories, remember directions.) Then practice doing some things you are learning.

Keep putting into practice all you learned.

PHILIPPIANS 4:9

Daniel and the Lions

DANIEL 6:1-28

There was a new king in the land where Daniel
and his friends were living. The new king liked
Daniel, just as the last king did.

Do you see Daniel waving?

The new king put Daniel in charge of many other leaders. Those leaders didn't like Daniel. They wanted to be more important than he was.

The wicked leaders wanted to get rid of Daniel. So they tried to find something that he was doing wrong. But they couldn't find anything! Daniel always did his work well, and everyone knew they could trust him. He did not lie or cheat. He was always kind and helpful.

One day one of the leaders said, "I know what we can do. We'll get Daniel in trouble for praying to God three times every day." So the leaders went to see the king.

The men told the king, "We think you should make a new law. Give orders that say everyone must pray only to you, O King. People must not pray to any other person or any god. If they do, they will be thrown into a den full of mean lions."

The king thought this sounded like a good idea. He smiled to himself. He thought that it would be very nice if all the people in his kingdom would have to pray to him, the king. So he said, "Okay. Let's do it!"

One of the king's helpers wrote down the new law. It said that everyone had to pray to the king. The people could not pray to any other person or any god. If they did, they would be thrown into a den of lions.

The king read the new law. He liked it, so he signed it. Now everyone would be ordered to obey the law. It was a law that could not be changed.

Daniel heard about the law. But he knew that it was a wicked law. He knew that God would not want him to obey it. So Daniel went home and stood by the window in his room. That's where he always prayed to God three times every day. And that's where he kept on praying three times every day.

The wicked leaders watched Daniel. They saw him pray to God. So they told the king about it. They said, "Daniel is praying to God. Your law says that he can pray only to you, O King. So Daniel must be thrown into a den of lions."

The king was upset, because he liked Daniel. He didn't want Daniel to be hurt by some mean lions. But there was nothing the king could do. His law could not be changed. So that night, the king had to let his soldiers throw Daniel into a den of mean lions. Then the soldiers put a big stone over the opening into the den.

Suddenly, the lions stopped roaring. God had sent an angel to shut the lions' mouths so they couldn't hurt Daniel! God had heard Daniel's prayers, and now he was keeping Daniel safe.

The king couldn't sleep that night. He was worried about Daniel.

Early the next morning the king hurried to the lions' den. A soldier moved the stone away, and the king called down to Daniel, "Was God able to save you?"

"Yes," said Daniel. "I'm okay. God sent an angel to keep the lions from hurting me. God's angel shut the lions' mouths! He kept me safe."

How happy the king was! He ordered his soldiers to lift Daniel out of the lions' den.

Everyone could see that Daniel didn't even have a scratch on him.

Look at the lions' mouths. Are they open or closed? God's angel closed the lions' mouths so the lions couldn't hurt Daniel.

The king wrote a letter to all the people in his kingdom. He said that everyone should worship Daniel's God. "He is a living God!" said the king. "He was able to save Daniel from the powerful lions."

Family Time

* Talk about why some wicked leaders wanted to get rid of Daniel.

* What did the leaders know that Daniel did three times every day?

* Recall the law that the leaders talked the king into signing.

* Did Daniel stop praying to God?

* Talk about what God did to help Daniel when he was thrown into a den of mean lions.

* When the king saw that Daniel was safe, what did the king tell the people of his kingdom to do?

Talk

A SAFE LION

Materials: a paper plate,
yellow or brown tissue paper, a paintbrush, yellow
paint, a brown crayon, scissors, and glue

To make a lion, paint the paper plate yellow. Then
cut the tissue paper into strips. When the plate
is dry, glue the strips of tissue paper around it.
Draw the lion's eyes, nose, mouth, and whiskers.
Whenever we feel afraid, we can ask God
to keep us safe.

Remember

**I prayed to the LORD, and he . . .
freed me from all my fears.**

PSALM 34:4

Jonah and the Great Fish

JONAH 1:1–4:11

God had a job for Jonah to do. But Jonah did not want to do it. So he ran away. Do you see Jonah running as fast as he can?

God wanted Jonah to go to the city of Nineveh. He wanted Jonah to warn the people there that they would be in big trouble if they didn't start obeying God's commands.

Do you know who the people of Nineveh were?
They were enemies of Jonah, who was from the land
of Israel. Jonah and the other Israelites worshiped
God. The people of Nineveh did not.

Jonah knew he should obey God
and go to teach the people of Nineveh
to obey God too. But Jonah didn't
want to do it.

201

Jonah hurried to get on a boat. The boat
was going to sail way to the west. But Nineveh,
where God wanted Jonah to go, was way to
the east.

God knew all about Jonah, just as he knows
all about everyone. He knew what Jonah was
going to do even before he did it. So God knew
that Jonah was going to try to hide from him.

Jonah got on the boat. He thought to himself,
"I'm safe now. God will never find me here."

But God did find Jonah. In fact, God knew all along exactly where Jonah was. God saw Jonah hiding in the bottom of the boat. So God made the wind blow hard. He sent a storm that made the little boat rock back and forth on the big waves.

The captain of the boat woke Jonah.

"Get up and pray," the captain said to Jonah. Jonah woke up and saw the storm. Right away, he knew that it was God who had sent the storm. The sailors looked at Jonah. They asked him, "Where are you from? Who are you? And what have you done? Did God send this storm because of you?"

"I am from the land of Israel," said Jonah. "I worship God, who created heaven and earth. He made the sea and the land. But I have been trying to run from him. I didn't want to obey him."

The storm was getting worse, and the sailors were afraid. They asked Jonah, "What can we do to stop this storm? We'll never get out of here alive if we don't do something soon."

Jonah told the sailors to throw him into the sea. So they did. And the storm stopped! Do you know how God kept Jonah safe? God sent a giant fish to swallow Jonah! Do you see where Jonah is?

What do you suppose Jonah did when he found himself inside the giant fish? He prayed! He said to God, "Thank you for sending the fish to save me. I'm sorry I tried to run from you. I won't do that again. I will obey you and do what you want me to do."

God was pleased that Jonah was ready to obey him. So God gave the giant fish orders to spit Jonah out onto the beach. Then God said to Jonah, "Get up and go to the city of Nineveh. Tell the people to obey me."

This time Jonah obeyed God and went to the city of Nineveh. He told the people there to obey God.

The people of Nineveh were sorry about the bad things they had done. They stopped doing bad things, and God forgave them. At first Jonah was upset that God forgave the people of Nineveh. But God taught Jonah that he always forgives people who are sorry for doing wrong.

Family Time

Talk

* Talk about why Jonah didn't like the people of Nineveh. Why didn't he obey God?

* Talk about why God sent a storm.

* What did the sailors do to Jonah?

* How did God keep Jonah safe?

* Discuss what Jonah did when he found himself inside the fish.

* After the fish spit Jonah out, where did Jonah go?

A BIG FISH

Materials: a cardboard box large enough for a young child to fit in (perhaps a box from an appliance store), paints, a paintbrush, and sharp scissors

Cut an entrance in one end of the box. Paint the box blue and silver or gray so it looks like a large fish. Paint the eyes, fins, and scales. When the fish is ready, go inside. Does God know where you are? Will he help you get out of the big fish? God knows all about you and will be with you even if you don't want him to know where you are.

Remember

LORD, you . . . know everything about me.
PSALM 139:1

NEW
TESTAMENT

Joseph and Mary

MATTHEW 1:18-25; LUKE 1:26-38

Joseph was working in his carpenter shop in the
city of Nazareth. He made things from wood. Do
you see him with his saw? Joseph had a favorite
visitor. Do you see Mary in the picture?

Mary liked to visit Joseph. She knew that he was a good man.

Soon Mary and Joseph were going to be married. Then they could live in the same house, and they could be together day and night. Joseph would be Mary's husband, and Mary would be Joseph's wife.

Mary was thankful to God for Joseph and for the home they would share someday.

Mary went back to her own house, where she lived with her mother and father. She went to bed and slept well all night.

The next day, Mary had a special visitor. Can you see who it was? Yes, it was an angel! His name was Gabriel, and he had a message for Mary from God.

"God is with you," Gabriel said. Mary was afraid. She wasn't even brave enough to look at the angel.

"Don't be afraid," said Gabriel. "God wants me to tell you that he has chosen you to be the mother of his Son. He wants you to name him Jesus."

Then the angel said, "Jesus will be a special King. And his Kingdom will last forever."

The angel told Mary that God would be the Father
of her Son. Mary didn't understand everything the
angel had told her. But she said to the angel, "I will
do whatever God wants. I will trust him to make
everything you've said come true." Then the angel left.

Later, an angel told Joseph, "Take Mary to be your
wife. She will have a child who is God's Son. Name
him Jesus." So Joseph married Mary.

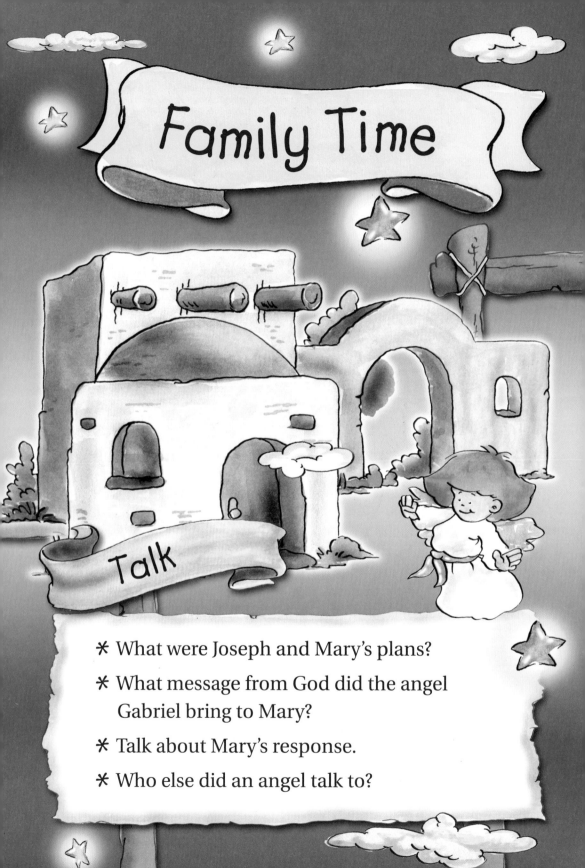

Family Time

Talk

* What were Joseph and Mary's plans?

* What message from God did the angel Gabriel bring to Mary?

* Talk about Mary's response.

* Who else did an angel talk to?

Do

NEWS FROM AN ANGEL

Look for pictures of angels in books and magazines. Then draw a picture to show how *you* think an angel looks.

Remember

[The angel told Mary,] "You will give birth to a son, and you will name him Jesus."

LUKE 1:31

Joseph, Mary, and Baby Jesus

LUKE 2:1-7

Mary and Joseph were on their way to Bethlehem, where Joseph was from. All of the people in the country had to be counted. They had to go to the place where their families had once lived.

Can you see what Mary was riding? It was a donkey! The trip was hard for Mary, because she was carrying baby Jesus inside of her. She knew that he would be born soon.

Joseph led the donkey that Mary was riding. He tried to make it go faster because he saw that Mary was tired. He wanted to look for a quiet, comfortable place to stay that night.

After many hours, Joseph and Mary came to Bethlehem. Most of the time, it was a quiet, little town. But not that day. Mary and Joseph heard noisy people and noisy animals everywhere.

People had come from all over the country to be counted in the town of Bethlehem. And all of those people needed a place to stay for the night.

Joseph went from door to door. He tried to find an inn that still had a room where he and Mary could sleep. But every place Joseph went, he heard the same words: "I'm sorry. Our inn is full. We have no more rooms for tonight."

Joseph didn't know what to do. Where would he and Mary sleep?

Then Joseph saw a small inn. He wondered if there might be a small room in the small inn where he and Mary could stay. He went to the door and knocked on it.

The innkeeper opened the door. Joseph asked, "Do you have a room where Mary and I can spend the night?" He told the innkeeper that Mary needed a place where she could rest. She was very tired, and her baby was going to be born soon.

The innkeeper shook his head. "No, I'm sorry. I have no rooms left. But you are welcome to stay in the stable where the animals are resting."

Do you see the innkeeper pointing to his stable? "It's quiet out there," he said. "And you'll be able to keep warm if you sleep on the hay."

"Thank you," said Joseph.

Mary and Joseph were glad that they finally had a place to stay. They didn't mind being with the cows and the sheep and the birds. Do you see the animals?

The animals in the stable were done eating. Now they were resting. And they quietly watched Mary and Joseph get ready for the night.

It was dark in Bethlehem. Everyone else in town was sleeping. But in the stable, it was still light.

During the night, Mary's baby boy was born. It was baby Jesus!

Mary wrapped baby Jesus in strips of cloth, and Joseph put some warm hay in a manger.

Mary laid baby Jesus in the manger. She looked
at her special baby with lots of love. So did Joseph.
So did the animals. God's Son was here!

Family Time

Talk

* Talk together about why Mary and Joseph had to go to Bethlehem.

* Talk about why Joseph walked and Mary rode a donkey. Discuss the fact that there were no cars, buses, trains, or airplanes.

* What was Joseph looking for in Bethlehem?

* Talk about the place Joseph finally found. Explain that the stable was like a barn where animals live. And the manger was like an open box where animals could eat hay. But the animals had finished eating, so the manger was a safe place for baby Jesus.

* Why was Mary's baby so special?

TIME TO WORSHIP AT THE MANGER

Materials: a baby doll, a small box, paper strips or yellow confetti, long robes, towels, and yarn or string

Fill a small box, such as a shoe box, with paper strips or yellow confetti. Place a baby doll in the box. Dress in long robes, with a towel for each person's head. Secure the towels with yarn or string. Then gather at the "manger" and take turns thanking God for sending his Son, Jesus.

> **[Mary] laid him in a manger.**
> **LUKE 2:7**

Remember

The Shepherds and Baby Jesus

LUKE 2:8-20

On the night when Jesus was born, shepherds were out in the fields with their sheep. Do you see the shepherd boy keeping warm by a fire?

The shepherds stayed awake so they could watch their sheep and keep them safe. The shepherds made sure that no mean animals came near to hurt the sheep while they were sleeping.

All of a sudden, there was an angel in the sky!

T[...]
got v[...]
all arou[...]
shepherds. They were afrai[...]
The angel said, "Don't be afraid! I have good
news that's going to make everyone happy. God's
Son has been born in Bethlehem! You'll find the
baby wrapped in cloth and lying in a manger."

Then a big choir of angels filled the sky. They
praised God together. "Glory to God in heaven, and
peace on earth to all who please him."

Before long, the angels went back to heaven. After they left, it was dark and quiet again.

The shepherds looked at one another. They wondered if angels had really visited them. But, of course, it was true. All the shepherds had seen and heard the angels. So they said to each other, "Let's go to Bethlehem. Let's find the baby who is God's Son."

The shepherds hurried into the little town of Bethlehem. It didn't take them long to find Mary and Joseph, who were awake in a stable. And there, sleeping quietly in a manger, was baby Jesus.

When the shepherds saw the baby, they knew that everything the angel had said was true. God had sent his Son, baby Jesus, to earth.

After they saw the baby, the shepherds went back to their sheep. And along the way, they told everyone the good news about baby Jesus!

Family Time

Talk

* Talk about what made some shepherds afraid one night.

* Talk about what the first angel said and what the big choir of angels said.

* After the shepherds found baby Jesus, what did they do?

AN ANGEL CHOIR

Materials: large, white T-shirts; aluminum foil; and worship music

Dress your whole family in large, white T-shirts, and make halos from rolled strips of foil. Have an older child or adult read the words the angel said in the story. Then listen to some favorite worship music and sing along. Thank God for sending an angel choir. Thank him for letting a group of shepherds know that Jesus had been born.

Remember

[The angel said,] "I bring you good news that will bring great joy to all people."

LUKE 2:10

Wise Men and Little Jesus

MATTHEW 2:1-12

Some wise men lived at the time when Jesus was born, but they lived far away from Bethlehem. They lived in a place that was in the East.

The wise men read about the stars and learned their names. At night, they studied the sky.

One night they saw a new star in the sky. They knew it meant that a special King had been born.

Can you see the new star in the sky?

The wise men decided to follow the star. Each of them took along a gift for the baby King.

The men had to travel a long way. They had to go across a hot, dry desert. Do you see what they rode? Yes, they rode on big camels!

The wise men traveled on their camels many days and nights. They kept following the special star. They were sure that it would lead them to the new little King who had been born.

At last the men on camels came to Jerusalem.
That's where wicked King Herod lived.

The wise men asked people about the baby King.
They said they wanted to worship him.

When King Herod heard about this, he was upset.
He wanted to be the only king. He didn't want a
baby to grow up and become a king too.

Herod talked to his helpers. He asked them,
"Where was the baby King supposed to be born?"

The king's helpers told him, "The baby King was
supposed to be born in Bethlehem."

King Herod said, "Tell the men from the East to come and see me." So the wise men met with wicked King Herod. He asked them when they first saw the new star in the sky.

Then Herod told the wise men, "Go to the town of Bethlehem, and look for the child. When you find him, come back here and tell me where he is. I want to go and worship him too."

That's what King Herod said. But that's not what he was thinking. He was thinking about how he could get rid of the new little king. He didn't want Jesus to grow up and become the King over all other kings—especially not over him, King Herod!

The wicked king pointed toward Bethlehem. So the wise men got back on their camels. They followed the star again. This time it led them to Bethlehem, to the house where little Jesus was.

How happy the wise men were to see little Jesus and his mother, Mary! They worshiped Jesus, who was the new King. And they offered him their gifts. Do you see the wise men's gifts?

They gave Jesus gifts that were just right for a king. They gave him bright, shiny *gold*. They gave him sweet-smelling *incense*, which was like perfume. And they gave him a spicy body lotion that was called *myrrh*.

When it was time for the wise men to leave, God told them in a dream that they should not go back to see King Herod. So they took a different route.

Instead of going back to Jerusalem, the wise men went right home to their own country in the East.

Talk

* Talk together about what the wise men saw in the sky and what the new star meant.

* Talk about where the wise men went and how they got there.

* What kind of king was Herod?

* What did the wise men do when they found little Jesus?

* Talk together about what the wise men did after they saw Jesus.

A GIFT FOR JESUS

Materials: pencils, drawing paper, a gift box, colorful wrapping paper, ribbon, and tape

Have each family member draw a big heart to give to Jesus. This will show him that you want to give him your love. Place your heart gifts in a box, and wrap it like a present. Set it out for a while as a reminder that you can give Jesus the gift of your love every day.

Remember

[The wise men] opened their treasure chests and gave him gifts.

MATTHEW 2:11

King Herod and Little Jesus

MATTHEW 2:13-15, 19-23

Do you see how mean and angry King Herod looks? He has learned that the wise men went home. He knows now that the wise men will not be coming to see him again.

"I told those wise men to come back and tell me where Jesus is! How can I get rid of Jesus if I don't know where he is? How can I keep him from growing up and taking my place as king?"

Herod came up with a plan. He would send soldiers to all the houses in Bethlehem. They would find Jesus for him.

But God had a plan too. He would keep Jesus safe.

Do you know what God did after the wise men left? God sent an angel to Joseph during the night. The angel talked to Joseph in a dream. Do you see Joseph in bed? Where is the angel?

The angel said to Joseph, "Get up right away. You must take little Jesus and his mother, Mary, to the land of Egypt. Stay there until I tell you that it is safe to come back."

Joseph woke up right away. He woke up Mary, too. And he told her what the angel had said.

Joseph and Mary quickly packed everything they would need for their trip to Egypt. Joseph rolled their things up in big bundles and put them on their donkey's back.

There was just enough room for two people to sit on the donkey too. Can you see who is sitting on the donkey? Yes, it is Mary and little Jesus!

It was still dark, because it was the middle of the night. Jesus was sleeping in Mary's arms as Joseph led the donkey out to the road that went to Egypt. Joseph ran as fast as he could. He pulled the donkey along, so the donkey had to run too.

Do you see the clouds of dust behind Joseph and behind the donkey? They were hurrying to the land of Egypt, where little Jesus would be safe from wicked King Herod and his soldiers.

Do you see the land of Egypt? Mary, Joseph, and little Jesus lived there until it was safe to go back to their own land. They waited until an angel came to Joseph in a dream again. "Now it is time for you to go home," said the angel. So the family went back home to the city of Nazareth.

Family Time

Talk

* Talk together about how God kept little Jesus safe from wicked King Herod.

* Where did Mary and Joseph and Jesus go?

* How did they know when it was safe to go home? Recall that "home" was Nazareth, where Mary and Joseph had lived before they went to Egypt.

MOVING TRUCK

Materials: construction paper, crayons, scissors, and tape

Mary and Joseph loaded their things onto a little donkey. Today we have moving trucks. Make a truck by cutting out a large rectangle and taping a small square to one side at the bottom. Draw a window on the small box. Then cut out two circles, and draw spokes to make wheels. Tape them to the bottom of the large rectangle— one at the left, the other at the right.

Remember

Lord, hurry to help me.

PSALM 70:1

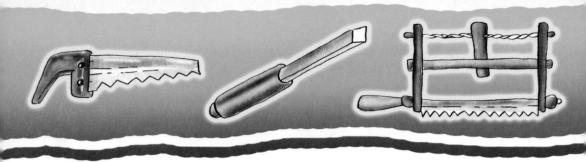

Jesus in Nazareth

LUKE 2:39-52

Jesus was no longer a baby. He was a boy living in the city of Nazareth. He lived with his mother, Mary, and with Joseph.

Jesus' Father was God, who lives in heaven. But his father on earth was Joseph. Jesus liked to help Joseph with his work.

Joseph was a carpenter. He made tables and chairs and cabinets and many other things from wood. Do you see Jesus in the carpenter shop?

Jesus played with his friends, just as you do. Can you see Jesus running after one of his friends in the picture? They look as if they are having a good time together, don't they?

But none of Jesus' friends knew who Jesus really was. They didn't know that God in heaven was his Father.

Jesus began to grow up. He became stronger and wiser. And God was with him.

One night when Jesus was 12 years old, he was
very excited. He didn't feel like going to sleep,
because he knew that the next day would be a
special day. He and his parents were going to start
out on a trip to Jerusalem.

The city of Jerusalem was where the Temple
was. Many other people would be traveling with
them. They would all go to worship God at the big,
beautiful Temple. Do you see the Temple?

Every year, people traveled from their homes to the city of Jerusalem. Many of them had to travel for several days.

This was the first year that Jesus could go to the Temple. That's because he had to be 12 years old before he could worship God there.

All of God's people liked to worship God at the Temple. But the building was even more special for Jesus. The Temple was God's house, and God was Jesus' Father!

After a week of worshiping and celebrating, it was time for everyone to go back home.

Mary and Joseph were with a big group of people who were walking back to Nazareth. They thought that Jesus was with some other family members or friends. But they soon found out that he was not anywhere in the group of travelers.

Mary and Joseph began to worry. Can you see how worried they were? They looked at each other and asked, "Where could Jesus be?" Then they said, "We must hurry back to the city of Jerusalem." So they did.

Where do you think Mary and Joseph found Jesus? They found him at the big, beautiful Temple! He was sitting with the teachers. He was listening to them and asking them questions. The teachers were amazed at how much Jesus knew. Do you see Jesus and the teachers?

Mary said, "Jesus! We have been looking for you everywhere. How could you do this to us?"

Jesus looked surprised. "Didn't you know I had to be here at the Temple—at my Father's house?"

Then Jesus went back to Nazareth with Mary and Joseph. He obeyed them and kept on growing bigger and wiser. God was pleased with his Son, Jesus. Everyone else liked him too.

* Talk together about some of the things Jesus did as he was growing up with Mary and Joseph in Nazareth.

* Talk about where the family went when Jesus was 12 years old.

* When Mary and Joseph didn't know where Jesus was, where did they finally find him?

* Why did Jesus like to be with the teachers at the Temple?

* Who did Jesus obey, and who was pleased with him?

Family Time

JUST LIKE JESUS

To become stronger just as Jesus did, play a running game, such as tag or hide-and-seek. To become wiser just as Jesus did, look at some pictures in this Bible, and see if you can remember the stories. To become obedient like Jesus, do what your parents ask you to do.

Remember

[Jesus] began to grow up. He became stronger and wiser.

LUKE 2:40

John the Baptist

MATTHEW 3:1-17; LUKE 3:3-18; JOHN 1:6-34

John and Jesus were cousins. Do you see John
standing by a river? John came from the desert.
He had been living alone out there. His clothes
were made from the hair of camels.

When John was living in the desert, he ate honey made by wild bees. And he ate locusts, which were like big grasshoppers!

Then John came to the Jordan River. He began preaching to people, telling them to be sorry about the bad things they had done.

John said, "Get ready for God's Son, Jesus. He is coming soon. He has come to save all people. He will pay for the bad things people have done."

Many came to hear John. They came from all over. They wanted to know if *he* was the one God had promised to send to them.

John said, "No, I'm not the one you've been waiting for. I am just pointing the way to him."

When people said they were sorry about the bad things they had done, John dipped them in the Jordan River. Then he brought them up out of the water. That's how he baptized them.

Because John baptized people, he was known as John the Baptist. Do you see the man in the picture who is being baptized by John the Baptist?

The water that washed the people on the outside showed that God also washed them on the inside.

God cleaned the hearts of the people and forgave them for the bad things they had done.

John talked to the people who said they were sorry about the bad things they had done. He said, "Don't just say you are sorry. *Show* you are sorry by the way you act."

"What should we do?" the people asked.

John answered, "Share your food with hungry people. Share your clothes with people who are poor. Be honest. Always tell the truth."

John told the people that someone was coming soon who was much greater than he was. "I'm not good enough to carry his sandals," said John. Of course, he was talking about Jesus.

This is my Son, whom I love. He brings me great joy.

One day Jesus came walking toward John the Baptist. John was so excited! He said, "Look! There is Jesus, God's Son! He is the one I've been telling you about. He came to take away all the bad things you do."

Jesus went to the Jordan River. He told John to baptize him. But John said, "You should baptize me."

"No," said Jesus. "You must baptize me. That is what God wants." So John the Baptist baptized God's Son, Jesus.

Do you see Jesus and John in the Jordan River?

When Jesus came up out of the water, something very special happened. The Spirit of God came down from heaven. God's Spirit looked like a dove.

John saw the dove from heaven. And he heard God say, "This is my Son, whom I love. He brings me great joy." Then John knew for sure that Jesus was God's very own Son.

Family Time

Talk

* Talk together about some of the things you've learned about John the Baptist.

* Talk about the people who were baptized by John and how he baptized them.

* When Jesus came to the Jordan River, what did he tell John to do?

* The Spirit of God came down from heaven when John baptized Jesus. What bird did he look like?

* What did John hear God say after Jesus was baptized?

THE DOVE

Materials: white poster board or a 4 x 6 index card, white tissue paper, a black crayon, white thread, a hole punch, and scissors

For the dove's body, draw an oval shape on white poster board or an index card. Draw tail feathers and a wedge shape for the head. Cut out the bird, and draw an eye on the head. Use scissors to cut a horizontal slit in the middle of the bird. Then accordion-fold a piece of tissue paper and pull it halfway through the slit for wings. Punch a hole at the top of the bird and use white thread to hang your dove where it can appear to fly like a real dove.

Remember

The Spirit looked like a dove and rested on [Jesus].

JOHN 1:33

Jesus and Nicodemus

JOHN 3:1-17

There was a group of men who were called Pharisees. They were important men who spent a lot of time reading Bible scrolls. Do you see the men reading the rolled-up Bible scrolls?

Most of those men didn't believe what the Bible says about Jesus. They didn't understand that Jesus is God's Son.

But one of the men knew that Jesus was special. That man's name was Nicodemus. And he wanted to learn more about Jesus.

So one night Nicodemus came to Jesus and said, "I know you are a teacher from God."

Jesus said, "I will teach you this: Everyone must start over and be born again."

"How can that be?" asked Nicodemus.

Jesus answered, "The first time you were born, you were a baby. And you became part of a family. Now you must believe in Me. If you do, you will become part of *God's* family."

Then Jesus said, "'God loved the world so much that he gave his one and only Son.' Someday, everyone who believes in God's Son will live with him forever in heaven."

Family Time

Talk

* Talk about the Pharisees and about the Bible scrolls that looked like paper-towel rolls.

* Discuss how these men read the first part of the Bible and learned that someone was coming to them from God. But they didn't believe that Jesus was this Person.

* Talk about how we become part of a family when we are born. Then we are born into God's family by believing in Jesus. It's like being born a second time!

* Why did God send his Son, Jesus, into the world?

* If we believe in Jesus, where will we live forever?

GOD'S LOVING HEART

Materials: red construction paper, a pencil, a gold or silver marker or pen, scissors, a hole punch, and red ribbon

Draw and cut out a heart from red construction paper, and print *God loves me!* on it in gold or silver. Punch a hole at the upper left and right. Pull the ribbon through the holes, tie it, and hang up the heart as a reminder that God loves the world and everyone in it!

Remember

God loved the world so much that he gave his one and only Son.

JOHN 3:16

Jesus and a Boat Full of Fish

MATTHEW 4:18-22; LUKE 5:1-11

Peter and his brother, Andrew, were fishermen. Can you see what they used to catch fish? They used a big net. That's Peter in the picture, looking at his net one night. Nighttime was supposed to be the best time to catch fish.

But do you see any fish in the net? No! Peter and Andrew fished from their boat in the middle of the lake all night. Fish were swimming in the water. But not one fish got caught in Peter and Andrew's net.

The brothers were upset. They needed to catch fish so they could sell them and earn some money.

In the morning Peter
and Andrew took their
boat back to shore. They
sat down on the sand and
began to mend their nets.
They washed the nets too.
The men wanted to be
ready again the next night
to try to catch some fish.

Then Jesus came. He
got into Peter's boat. Jesus
asked Peter to take the boat
out into the water. Jesus wanted to
talk to the big crowd of people who had come
to listen to him.

So Peter did what Jesus asked. And the big crowd
of people listened to Jesus talk about God, his Father
in heaven. Everyone could see Jesus and hear him as
he talked to them from the boat.

When Jesus finished preaching, he talked to Peter
again. "Go out to the middle of the lake. Put your nets
down into the water, and you will catch some fish."

Peter and his brother, Andrew, knew that daytime was not a good time to catch fish. But they did what Jesus told them to do.

The men let their nets down into the water. And what do you think happened? The nets were so full of fish that they started to tear! So Peter and Andrew called to their partners in another boat.

James and John came to help. They worked with Peter and Andrew to pull the heavy nets into the two boats. Both boats were soon filled with fish. The boats were almost ready to sink!

Peter knew that no one but Jesus could have found all of those fish. Jesus found them because he is God's Son.

Peter got down on his knees. He said, "Jesus, I'm not good enough to be close to you."

Jesus told Peter not to be afraid. He said, "Come, follow me, and I will show you how to fish for people! They will become part of my family."

Jesus chose Peter, Andrew, James, and John to be his first helpers.

Talk

* Talk about Bible-time fishermen. How did they fish? Why did they fish? When? Where?

* Why did Jesus need Peter's boat?

* When Jesus was in the boat with the fishermen, what happened when they caught so many fish?

* What new job did Jesus have for the fishermen to do?

* Who were the first four fishermen to follow Jesus and be his helpers?

THE FISH

Materials: white construction paper, a pencil, watercolors, colorful tissue paper, aluminum foil, glue, and scissors

Draw the shape of a fish similar to the one below. Cut it out and color it with watercolors. If you wish, decorate the fish with tissue paper or foil. God created many beautiful fish. But Jesus taught his helpers to find people instead of fish so the people could join God's family.

Remember

[Jesus said,] "Come, follow me, and I will show you how to fish for people!"

MATTHEW 4:19

Jesus and His Disciples

MATTHEW 4:23-25; 9:35-38; MARK 3:7-8, 13-19;
LUKE 6:12-20, 27-38; JOHN 13:33-35; 14:15, 23, 27

Jesus had a lot of work to do. He walked from one town to another, teaching people about God. And everywhere he went, many people followed him. Some of the people were sick. Some had a hard time walking. All of them wanted to be well.

The news about Jesus spread to many places. So people came from far away. They wanted to hear Jesus teach about God. And they wanted Jesus to help them.

Jesus loved the people. So he taught them about God. He made sick people well. And if their legs didn't work right, Jesus fixed them so they could walk just fine!

Jesus cared about those people, but he needed to find others who would care too. He already had four helpers. Can you name them?

Now Jesus climbed a mountain. He prayed for 12 men who would spend time with him and learn from him.

God helped his Son, Jesus, choose his 12 disciples.

Peter

Here are Jesus' 12 special helpers. Let's follow the arrow from each disciple's name to his picture.

Jesus began teaching his disciples the
right way to live. He said, "Love everyone.
And treat other people the way you
want them to treat you."

Jesus also said, "Care about other people and how they feel. Be kind to them so they will feel happy. Then you will be happy too.

"If someone makes you sad by being unkind, forgive that person. Don't get angry, and don't keep talking about what your friend did.

"If you love me, obey my commands," said Jesus. "Do what I tell you, and you will be happy.

"Someday I will leave. I will go back to heaven. After I leave, I want you to love one another." Point to the picture of Jesus and the heart. "Love one another the way I have loved you. Then everyone will know that you belong to me."

Family Time

Talk

* Talk together about the work Jesus did.

* Why did Jesus want to help people? (He loved them; he cared about them.)

* Talk about how Jesus prayed to his Father in heaven when he had important choices to make.

* What is another name for Jesus' 12 special helpers?

* Talk about some of the things Jesus wanted his disciples to do.

* Talk about how we can please Jesus just as his 12 disciples did. We show love for Jesus when we love one another.

PEOPLE WE CAN LOVE

Materials: photos of your child, other family members, and friends; pictures of more children from catalogs, magazines, and newspaper ads; scissors; glue; and construction paper

Make a collage of photos and pictures of various children and adults. Glue the pictures to a piece of construction paper. Identify the people you know in the photos. And name people you know whom you think the pictures look like. Talk about ways people can show love for one another. Explain that we learn from Jesus to show love to one another just as he shows love to us. And when we love one another, we show that we love Jesus.

Remember

[Jesus said,] "Learn from me."

MATTHEW 11:29

Jesus and a Sick Little Girl

LUKE 8:40-42, 49-56

A man named Jairus lived with his wife and his little girl. They lived in a town by a big lake. Jairus was a worship leader there.

Jairus and his little girl liked to walk together. As they walked, Jairus would tell stories.

One day, Jairus's little girl got sick. Jairus was upset because she wasn't getting better.

Jairus and his wife asked the doctor what to do for their daughter. The doctor told them that there was nothing they could do to help their little girl. And there was nothing he could do to help her either. Do you see the doctor talking to Jairus? Do you see how Jairus is covering his face? He is very sad.

Then Jairus remembered that Jesus was nearby. And he knew Jesus could make sick people well!

Jairus found Jesus by the lake. "Jesus, please come home with me," begged Jairus. "My little girl is sick. No one knows how to help her. But I know that you can help."

So Jesus went with Jairus to his house. Jesus wanted to help Jairus's little girl. And Jesus knew that he was the only one who could help.

As Jesus and his disciples walked with Jairus to the house where Jairus lived, a helper from Jairus's house met them on the road. The man was crying. He said to Jairus, "It's too late to help your little girl. Jesus doesn't need to come home with you. Even he can't help her now."

But Jesus said, "Don't be afraid, Jairus. Trust me." Jairus did trust Jesus. He believed that Jesus could still make his little girl well again.

So Jesus and his disciples kept on walking toward Jairus's house. When they got there, they saw many sad people. They were all crying.

Jesus went to the little girl's room. He took his three best friends—Peter, James, and John—with him. He took the little girl's parents—Jairus and his wife—with him too.

Jesus went over to the little girl's bed. She looked as if she was just sleeping. Jesus said to her, "Little girl, get up!" Right away the little girl opened her eyes and stood up!

The little girl was okay again. She was alive
and well. She began dancing around the room.
How happy her parents were! Their sadness was
gone. They had known all along that Jesus would
be able to help. But when he did, they could
hardly believe it.

"Give your little girl something to eat," Jesus said.
So they did. And their little girl ate everything they
gave her.

Once again, Jairus and his wife and his little girl
were a happy, healthy family. And all around them,
people began to talk about what Jesus had done.

Family Time

Talk

* Talk together about why Jairus went to see Jesus.

* Talk about which people in the story were crying. Do not frighten your child by focusing on the fact that children can die. Simply explain that Jesus can help people today who are very sick and very sad, just as he did in Bible times.

* What did Jesus do for the little girl and her parents?

BALLOON OF HAPPINESS

Materials: markers, and a balloon for each family member in his or her favorite color

Blow up the balloons. Then draw a sad face on one side and a happy face on the other. Turn the balloon from one side to the other as you say the verse below. When you feel sad, point to the sad faces on your balloons. When God helps you feel happy again, point to the happy faces.

Remember

I will change their sadness into happiness.

JEREMIAH 31:13

Jesus and the Children

MARK 10:1, 13-16

When Jesus walked from one place to another, many people followed him. Wherever a large crowd of people gathered, Jesus would stop and teach them about God and his love. Look at the picture. Do you see grown-up people? Do you see boys and girls?

The children came with their parents. But the children couldn't get near Jesus.

There were so many grown-ups listening to Jesus that the little children couldn't even see him. They were upset. And their parents were upset.

The moms and the dads wanted Jesus to hold their children and pray for them. But Jesus' disciples said, "Take your children and leave. Don't bother Jesus now. Can't you see that he is busy?"

Jesus heard what his helpers said. He was not happy with them. So Jesus told them, "Let the children come to me. Don't stop them." Then the disciples understood what Jesus wanted. And they told the crowd to make room for the children.

When the grown-ups moved out of the way, do you think the children were afraid to run up to Jesus? No! Look at the children who are running toward him. How many do you see? And look at the children who are sitting with Jesus. How many do you see there?

The boys and girls took turns sitting in Jesus' lap. As Jesus held the children, he placed his hands on their heads and prayed for them.

Jesus had plenty of time for each child. The boys and girls loved Jesus because they knew that he loved them. They all had important things to tell him, and he listened to each one.

Jesus had important things to tell the children, too. He told them about God, his Father in heaven. He told them how much God loved them.

The children's parents were nearby, watching and listening and smiling. Jesus' disciples and the other grown-ups from the big crowd were nearby too. Jesus said to all the grown-ups, "Anyone who wants to be in God's family must love God and trust him just like these boys and girls do."

What a wonderful day the children had with Jesus! He was the best Friend they'd ever had.

Family Time

Talk

* Talk together about why
  the children couldn't get close to Jesus at first.

* What did Jesus' disciples tell the parents?
  And what did Jesus say?

* Talk about what Jesus did when the children
  came to him.

* What did Jesus say grown-ups have to do
  in order to be in God's family?

PICTURE FOR JESUS

Materials: drawing paper and crayons

Have each family member draw a picture for Jesus—a picture of your family, your house, a pet, a flower, etc. Hang the drawings on your refrigerator. Point out that even though you can't see Jesus, he is in your home. You can pray to Jesus and tell him what you would say if you could sit on his lap like the children in the Bible story.

Remember

Let the little children come to me.

MARK 10:14

Jesus and 5,000 People

LUKE 9:10-17; JOHN 6:1-13

One morning a long line of people came walking along the lake. Do you see the people? Do you see the lake?

The people walked past a boy who was helping his father. The father and son were taking fish out of a net. Can you find the boy and his father, and the fish in the net? The man was a fisherman, and his son liked to help him.

The boy wondered where all the people were going. His father told him, "They are going to see Jesus."

"I want to see Jesus too," the boy said.

His father told him he could go and find Jesus. "But first," his father said, "you must ask your mother to fix a lunch for you."

So the boy ran to the house and asked his mother if she would please fix a lunch for him. Then he would go and find Jesus.

His mother fixed a lunch of bread and fish. She put the food in a basket. Then the boy ran to catch up with the crowd going to see Jesus.

Finally the boy saw Jesus sitting on a hillside. Jesus' helpers, the disciples, were with him. And a big crowd was listening to him. Jesus was teaching about God, his Father in heaven, just as he always did. The people listened all day long. They didn't even think about how hungry they were.

By now, it was getting late. Jesus' 12 helpers told him to send the crowds away so they could look for food.

But Jesus said, "No, you feed them."

The disciples knew they would never find enough food. More than 5,000 men and also women and children had come to hear Jesus that day.

But Andrew, one of Jesus' 12 disciples, found the boy whose mother had fixed him a lunch that morning. The boy had been so excited to see Jesus that he hadn't taken time to eat his lunch yet. So Andrew asked the boy, "Would you like to share your lunch?"

The boy looked around at all the people. "Sure," he said. "If you think it would help."

Andrew took the boy to see Jesus. "Here is a boy with five loaves of bread and two fish," said Andrew. Can you count the five loaves? Where are the two fish?

"It's not a very big lunch," said Andrew.

But Jesus was smiling at the little boy. He saw how happy the boy was to give what he had. So Jesus took the boy's basket with the five loaves of bread and the two fish in it.

Jesus told his helpers, the disciples, to have everyone sit down on the grass. Then Jesus took the five loaves of bread and thanked God for them. He had his helpers give bread to the 5,000 men and to all the women and children.

Jesus thanked God for the fish, too. And the disciples gave fish to the 5,000 men and all the women and children, too.

The people ate as much as they wanted. And there were even leftovers! Jesus' helpers gathered 12 baskets of leftovers!

The little boy was so happy that he had given his lunch to Jesus. He had watched Jesus turn that little lunch into a big picnic lunch for everyone! Only Jesus could have done that.

When the boy went home to his family, he had exciting news for them. He told them all about the hungry crowd of people. And he told them that Jesus had used his basket of lunch to feed everyone!

Family Time

Talk

* Talk together about the lunch the little boy brought. What was in it, and how many was it supposed to feed?

* Talk about the hungry crowd of people and all the food they needed.

* If you had been the little boy with the lunch, do you think you would have given it to Jesus? Would you have been happy to give it to him?

* Talk together about what Jesus did that was unusual. Could anyone else but Jesus turn one little lunch into enough food for more than 5,000 people?

* How much food was left over?

Do

FOOD TO SHARE

Materials: bread or crackers, tuna salad or peanut butter and jelly, grapes or an apple, and milk or juice

Choose a snack to make for yourself and a friend. Work together to make the snack. Then see how much fun you can have when you happily share what you have with someone else.

Remember

God loves the person who gives happily.
2 CORINTHIANS 9:7

Jesus and Prayer

MATTHEW 6:9-13; 7:7-11

One day Jesus taught his followers how to talk to God. Jesus' prayer is called the Lord's Prayer because Jesus is our Lord. He is the one we love and want to obey. We can use these words of Jesus to pray to God, who is *our* heavenly Father too!

Our Father in heaven, we pray that your name will always be kept holy. We pray that your Kingdom will come. We pray that what you want will be done here on earth as it is in heaven. Give us the food we need for each day. Forgive the bad things we have done, just as we forgive those who have done wrong to us. Do not let us be tested, but save us from the evil one.

Jesus also said that you should keep asking God for the things you need. And he will give you what is best for you. If you asked your mother or father for a piece of bread, would your mom or dad give you a stone to eat? Of course not! Your parents know what is good for you. And God knows even more than they do. Jesus said, "Your heavenly Father will give good things to those who ask him."

Talk

* Talk about what Jesus teaches us to include in our prayers.

* Talk about what it means to keep asking. Explain that we can ask for anything, but God gives us what he knows is best for us.

* Talk about ways parents show how they know what is best for their children. For example, if we ask them for cookies or candy for breakfast, they will probably give us cereal instead.

* Who knows even more than our parents?

PRAYING HANDS

Materials: construction paper
in different colors, a pencil, scissors, and paste

Let each family member choose a color of
construction paper. On the papers, trace around
both hands of each person and cut them out.
Paste the hands together so they look as if they
are praying hands. Print each person's name
on his or her hands. Then suggest that your
family members keep their praying hands in a
place where they will see them each day and
remember to pray.

Remember

**Your heavenly Father will give good
things to those who ask him.**

MATTHEW 7:11

Two Builders

MATTHEW 7:24-29; LUKE 6:46-49

One day Jesus told a story about the houses that two men built. Only one of the men was a wise builder. The other man was a foolish builder.

The wise builder knew what he was doing. The foolish builder didn't think things through. Nothing he did made any sense.

Do you see the man with the brown hair? He was the wise builder who knew what he was doing. Let's look at the house he built. He found a good spot to build his house. He built it on a big, flat rock. Do you see the rock? He built the house from strong materials. And he built it on a safe place. It would never slide off the big rock.

When the rain came down and the wind blew hard, the wise man's house stood tall. It didn't move, and it didn't fall.

But then there was the foolish builder. He was the man with a beard. Do you see him?

The foolish builder didn't think things through.
He built his house on sand. Do you see the sand?
He did not build his house from strong materials.
And he did not build it on a safe place. It could
easily fall down in the sand. And if there was a long,
hard rain, the house could sink down into the water.
This was not a good place to live.

When the rain came down and the wind blew
hard, what do you think happened to this house?

Crash! Bam! The foolish man's house fell flat. It
was gone—just like that!

The wise builder still had his house after the storm was gone. Do you see it? But the foolish builder didn't have a house anymore.

Jesus said that we should not be like the foolish builder. We should be like the wise builder. To be like him, we must do two things. We must *listen* to what Jesus teaches us in the Bible. And we must *obey* him. Then we can live with Jesus forever. We'll always have a safe place to live.

Family Time

* Talk about what happened to the wise man's house when the wind blew hard and the rain came down.

* Talk about what happened to the foolish man's house when the wind blew hard and the rain came down.

* Which builder do you want to be like?

* What two things did Jesus say we need to do if we want to be like the wise builder?

Talk

THE HOUSES

Materials: sand in a sandbox or at the beach, a pail of water, and plastic interlocking blocks with a solid base

Make a house from sand. Then pour a pail of water over it. You'll see how it falls flat—just like that! Build another house from plastic blocks on a solid base. After you pour water on it, exclaim that your house stood tall. It didn't move; it didn't fall! If we want to be as happy and as wise as the wise builder, we'll listen to the Bible (the Word of God) and obey it.

Remember

Blessed . . . are those who hear the word of God and obey it.

LUKE 11:28

The Good Samaritan

LUKE 10:25-37

One day Jesus told a story about a man who was traveling from one place to another. The man had left the city of Jerusalem. And he was on his way down the rocky hillsides to the town of Jericho.

The traveler was hot and tired. Do you see him riding his camel? The town of Jericho was not very far away. But there were no smooth roads. So the man couldn't travel very fast.

Then, all of a sudden, two mean-looking men came out from behind a bush. Do you see the two men? They were robbers. They beat up the man who was going to Jericho. Then they took the man's money and everything else he had.

The robbers ran away and left the man lying by the side of the road.

Do you see the man who was robbed? The robbers had hurt him so much that he couldn't stand up. He couldn't even call for help.

Then the man heard footsteps. *Oh, that's good,* the man thought to himself. *Someone is here to stop and help me.*

Someone *was* there. It was a priest from the Temple in Jerusalem. But do you know what he did? The priest pretended he didn't see the man who had been hurt. He walked right by him.

The beat-up man wondered if anyone else would come down the road. Someone else *did* come. He was a helper at the Temple in the city of Jerusalem. Do you see the helper? Where is the hurt man?

The Temple helper did not help at all. He walked over and looked at the hurt man but didn't do anything for him. He just started walking away. He began walking faster and faster.

The hurt man felt all alone. It looked as if no one was going to stop and help him.

Then a man from another country came along.
He was a Samaritan. The hurt man saw him and
thought to himself, *Oh no. That man is an enemy.
He will never stop and help me.*

But the man who had been robbed and hurt was wrong. The Samaritan man *did* stop. And he *did* help the hurt man. Can you see what the Samaritan man was riding? He was riding a donkey, wasn't he?

Can you tell what the Samaritan man is doing in the small picture? He is giving the hurt man some water to drink. The Samaritan man also cleaned up the hurt man's sore places. He put oil on them and covered them with bandages.

Then the Samaritan man got his donkey and put the hurt man on it. He said, "We're going to find an inn where you can stay until you are well again."

And that is just what the Samaritan man did.

Do you know where the hurt man is in this picture? He's in a nice, comfortable bed. The bed is in a room that the Samaritan man rented.

The Samaritan stayed with the hurt man at the inn all night. He gave the man water to drink. And he kept the man covered up so he would be warm.

The next day the Samaritan man paid for the room at the inn. He also gave some more money to the man who owned the inn.

He said, "This man has been robbed and hurt. Use the money to care for him. I will come back and pay you more money if the bill is more than this."

Jesus told the story about the Good Samaritan to teach us that we can be good neighbors too. We can help people just like the Good Samaritan did. We can help people close by. And we can help people far away. They are all our neighbors. If we help them, we show God that we love them. We also show the people that we love them.

Family Time

* Talk together about what happened to the man who was traveling.

* Talk about how sad the hurt man was when two people didn't help.

* Talk about all the ways the Good Samaritan showed love for the man who had been robbed and hurt.

* Identify neighbors who live close by and others who live far away. According to Jesus' story, is there anyone who is not like a neighbor?

Talk

Do

GOOD SAMARITANS

Materials: a washcloth, a small pan of soapy water, adhesive bandages, and coins

Use the above items to act out the story of the Good Samaritan. Then plan a way your family can help a close neighbor and someone else far away.

Remember

Love your neighbor as yourself.

LUKE 10:27

The Lost Son

LUKE 15:11-24

Jesus liked to tell stories. This story is about a father and two sons. Where is the father? Where are the two sons?

Jesus told the story to teach us that God is like the father.

This man loved both of his sons. But the two sons were very different from each other. They looked different, they talked and behaved differently, and different things made them happy.

The older son was happy to live with his family. He worked hard on the family farm. And he did whatever his father asked him to do.

The younger son was not happy. He wanted to leave home. So he asked his father for money he should not have had until after his father died. "I want my money now," he said.

The father felt sad. He didn't want his son to leave. His son already had everything he needed.

But the father agreed to give his younger son the money he wanted.

"I will give you your money," said the wise father. "You have the right to do what you want to do."

So the younger son took the money and left. Can you see how far away he is already?

The sad father watched his son get farther and farther away. The sad father called to his son, "You can always come back to me. I will always wait for you."

But the son didn't even look back and wave to his father.

The young man found some new friends. He bought a lot of things for them with the money his father had given him. He invited them to some wild parties, and he paid for all the food and drinks.

But before long, the young man had no more money. He had not been working to make more. He had just been spending all his money.

After the money was gone, the young man's friends left too.

The friends were not real friends. They hung around when the young man had money to spend on them. They liked being invited to his parties. And they liked the gifts he gave them.

But when the young man needed food to eat and clothes to wear, his new friends would not help him. Do you see the young man's raggedy clothes? When he asked for money to buy food and clothes, his friends said, "Go away."

The young man looked for a job. He thought, *Maybe I can work for a farmer who lives nearby.* So he talked to a farmer. He told the farmer that he had no money. He said he needed a job. The farmer did what he could to help. He sent the young man out to feed the pigs. How many pigs do you see in the picture? They look like they have had plenty to eat, don't they?

The young man was so hungry that he wanted to eat the food the pigs were eating! But no one gave him any food.

Finally the young man said to himself, *At home, the men who work for my father have plenty to eat. But I don't have any food. I'm going home! I'll tell my father that I'm sorry I left home and spent his money. I'll ask him to please forgive me and let me come back. I won't expect to be his son. I'll be one of his workers.*

So the young man began the long walk back home to his father.

When the young man got closer to the house, who do you think he saw standing in the doorway? It was his father! Do you see him?

Every day since his son left home, the father had been watching and waiting for him to come back. Now the father was filled with love and happiness as his son came down the road toward him. Do you know what the father did? He ran out to meet his son! And he gave his son a big hug!

The son got down on his knees and hugged his father. "I'm so sorry," he said. "I have done many wrong things. May I come home as a worker?"

The father said, "No, you will not just be a worker. You will be my son again. You were lost, but now you are back home."

The father had his workers bring out fine clothes for his son. He gave his son a ring for his finger and sandals for his feet. He had his workers get a big party ready, with a lot of food.

God loves us just as the lost son's father loved him. And God forgives us when we're sorry for the wrong things we do. He will never stop loving us.

Family Time

* Talk about what the younger son asked his father to give him.

* Recall what the younger son did with his money.

* What happened to the young man after his money was gone?

* Talk about how the young man showed he was sorry. Then review how the father showed love and forgiveness to his son.

Talk

A PICTURE STAND

Materials: clay or Play-Doh; a wooden craft stick (e.g., a Popsicle stick); a photo of you and your father, grandfather, big brother, neighbor, or church friend

Take a big lump of clay or Play-Doh and press it until it becomes soft. Shape it the way you would like it. You might make a star or a crown. Be sure it has a thick, flat bottom. Make a long slit in the bottom with a craft stick. Then stand up your photo in the slit. God loves you even more than your father does [or your grandfather or big brother or anyone else]!

Remember

O Lord, you are so good, so ready to forgive.

PSALM 86:5

Jesus, the Good Shepherd

LUKE 15:1-7; JOHN 10:1-16

One day, Jesus told a story about sheep and their shepherds. Sheep need a shepherd to take care of them the same way boys and girls and even grown-ups need someone to take care of *them*.

Jesus told this story to teach us that he is like a shepherd and we are like sheep. Let's see how the shepherd in the story takes care of his sheep.

There was a shepherd who had 100 sheep. How many of them do you see in the picture? What is the shepherd holding? He has a baby sheep, doesn't he? It's called a lamb.

The shepherd led his sheep to a place where there was a lot of grass for them to eat. The sheep followed him because they knew him. And they knew his voice. They trusted him. Can you see how happy the sheep were? They were happy because there was plenty of grass for all of them.

The shepherd stayed in the green field with his sheep as long as they wanted to keep eating grass. He watched the sheep. And the sheep felt safe. They knew that their shepherd wouldn't leave them.

When the sheep had eaten all the grass they
wanted, their shepherd led them to a place where
they could drink all the water they wanted.

Do you see how the shepherd piled up some
stones? He put the stones there so that the water
wouldn't run too fast. He didn't want his sheep to
be afraid. And he didn't want them to get hurt.

The sheep were thirsty. They drank and drank.
They were glad that their shepherd knew where
to find water for them to drink.

But one day a big, black wolf jumped out from behind some bushes where he had been hiding. Do you think the shepherd ran away? Did he let the wolf get near his sheep? No! Of course not!

Look at what the shepherd is doing in the picture. He is going after the wolf. And he's hitting the wolf with his shepherd's stick.

That wolf knew it was time to get out of there! So he turned around and ran away as fast as he could. He knew better than to stay and get hurt by a shepherd.

When it was evening, the shepherd led his sheep back to their pen. They would be safe there all night.

The sheep went into their pen, and their shepherd counted them as he always did. One, two, three . . . all the way up to 99. But there should have been 100. One lamb was missing!

It was dark, and the shepherd was tired. But he couldn't go to bed. He had to find the missing lamb. So he took his shepherd's stick to help him walk and a lamp to help him see.

He looked for a long time. Finally, he heard a soft little *Baa, baa.*

How excited the shepherd was! He had found his missing lamb! He picked up the little sheep and carried it home on his shoulders. Then he called to his neighbors and said, "Let's have a party! I found my lost sheep!"

Wasn't that a good story? The best part about it is that it's a story about Jesus! We can follow him the way sheep follow their shepherd. Jesus said, "I am the good shepherd. I know my own sheep, and they know me."

Family Time

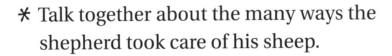

Talk

✴ Talk together about the many ways the shepherd took care of his sheep.

✴ Talk about why the sheep followed their shepherd.

✴ How many sheep did the shepherd have? Talk about how the shepherd showed love for the one little lamb that was lost.

✴ Jesus is the Good Shepherd. Who are we? How does Jesus care for us?

LIKE A SHEEP

Materials: pencil, white or pink construction paper, scissors, glue, cotton balls, and two spring-type clothespins

Draw and cut out a large oval for your sheep's body. Glue on a medium-size oval for the head, and three small ovals for ears and a tail. Then glue cotton balls to your sheep and attach two clothespins for legs.

Remember

I am the good shepherd; I know my own sheep, and they know me.

JOHN 10:14

Jesus on top of the Water

MATTHEW 14:22-33; MARK 6:45-52

Late one afternoon Jesus told his helpers, the disciples, to get into their boat. He told them to go across the lake to the other side.

After his helpers sailed away, Jesus walked up into the hills. He went there by himself. He wanted to pray.

342

Before long, the sun went down. Soon it was dark. The disciples were in their boat in the middle of the lake. And Jesus was still praying on a hillside.

The wind began to blow hard, and big waves splashed against the boat. Do you see the boat? Do you see the waves?

Jesus' helpers were afraid. They had to take their sails down and use their oars. Point to the sails and the oars.

The disciples used their oars to row as hard as they could. But they couldn't get to the shore on the other side of the lake. Oh, how they wished Jesus was with them! They knew he would be able to help them.

The wind began to blow harder and harder. "Where is Jesus? Oh, where is he?" they asked.

Do you see where Jesus was? At three o'clock in the morning, Jesus came toward his disciples in the boat. And look! He was walking on top of the water! He wasn't swimming. He was walking. But he didn't sink.

At first, Jesus' helpers thought he was a ghost. They had never seen a real, live person walk on top of the water.

But then they heard Jesus say, "Don't be afraid. I am here." And the disciples wondered if the man walking on water really was Jesus.

Peter called out, "Jesus, is it really you? If it is, I want to walk over to you on top of the water."

"Come," said Jesus.

So Peter began walking on the water. He took one step, and then another. But when he looked at the big waves around him, he got scared. And then he began to sink. "Save me, Jesus!" he said.

Can you see how Jesus is helping Peter? Jesus reached out to him and pulled him up.

"Why were you afraid?" asked Jesus. "Didn't you believe that I could help you?"

Jesus held on to Peter and helped him get back to the boat. As soon as they were in it, the wind stopped blowing, and the waves gently rocked the boat from side to side.

Jesus' helpers, the disciples, were not afraid anymore. Jesus was with them, and they knew they were safe.

The disciples worshiped Jesus. They knew now that no one was as special as he was. No one but Jesus could walk on top of the water.

"Oh, Lord Jesus," they said. "You really are the Son of God."

Family Time

* Talk together about why the disciples in the boat were afraid during a storm.

* Why did Jesus go up into the hills?

* What did the disciples see Jesus doing at three o'clock in the morning?

* Talk about how unsafe it would be for any of us to try to walk on top of water. Focus on the fact that only Jesus, God's Son, could do that.

* Talk about what happened when Peter tried to walk on top of the water. How did Jesus help Peter?

* Why did the disciples worship Jesus?

STAND OR SINK

Materials: a large tub or pan, water, a washcloth, plastic action figures, bathtub toys, and a towel

Wash your action figures and tub toys. Check to see which items float and which ones sink. Then take turns seeing if anyone in your family can stand on top of the water. You'll discover that people are not made to stand on top of water. They don't float. They sink. But Jesus could walk on water because he is God's Son.

Remember

Jesus came toward them, walking on the water.

MARK 6:48

Zacchaeus and Money

LUKE 19:1-10

A rich man named Zacchaeus lived in the city of
Jericho. Zacchaeus doesn't look very happy, does
he? Do you know why? He had no friends.

Zacchaeus was a tax collector. Every day he sat by his box of money. And every day he took money from people for their taxes.

Being a tax collector wasn't wrong. But Zacchaeus cheated people, and that wasn't right. He made them give him more money for the king than the king wanted them to give.

If someone was supposed to pay one gold coin, Zacchaeus would say, "Give me two coins." One coin would go into the box for the king. But the other coin would go into Zacchaeus's pocket.

That's why no one liked Zacchaeus. Can you see how upset the man in the picture is?

One day Zacchaeus learned that Jesus was coming to town. Zacchaeus had heard that Jesus was an amazing teacher. He had heard that Jesus could do things no one else could do. But even more important, Jesus taught people that God loved them and would forgive them for the bad things they did.

Zacchaeus was a short man. He was shorter than everyone else. Can you find him? Do you see all the people waiting for Jesus?

Zacchaeus couldn't get through the big crowd of people to see Jesus. *What can I do?* he asked himself. *I know that no one likes me, so no one will let me through.*

Oh, how Zacchaeus wanted to see Jesus! He wished that he and Jesus could be friends. The short man ran ahead of the crowd and climbed up into a tree. He thought that maybe he would be able to see Jesus walking down the road.

Before long, the crowd of people came walking down the road. They were listening to Jesus. He was teaching them about his Father in heaven.

Zacchaeus looked down from the tree. There was Jesus! Zacchaeus could see him. And he could hear him teach about God, his Father.

The people with Jesus saw Zacchaeus in the tree. But they hoped Jesus wouldn't see him. They didn't think Jesus would want to talk to a man like Zacchaeus.

But Jesus stopped under the tree where Zacchaeus was. Then Jesus looked up and said, "Zacchaeus, come down from that tree. I want to visit with you at your house today!"

The people in the crowd couldn't believe that Jesus wanted to go home with Zacchaeus. They thought to themselves, *Doesn't Jesus know that the man cheats us out of our money?*

But Jesus did know. And that was exactly why Jesus wanted to visit with the man in the tree.

Zacchaeus was even more surprised than the other people. Why would Jesus want to come to his house?

But Zaccheus climbed down the tree as fast as he could. He wanted to be sure that Jesus didn't change his mind. He thought to himself, *Jesus called me by my name! He knows my name! He knows who I am! I want to take him to my house for a long visit.*

356

As soon as Zacchaeus saw Jesus, he felt sorry about all the bad things he had done. He said, "Jesus, I'm going to give half of my money to people who have no money. And if I have taken too much money from people for their taxes, I'll give them back four coins for every coin I should not have taken."

Jesus smiled. He said, "I came to help people like this man. Now he belongs to God's family."

Family Time

* Talk together about why Zacchaeus had no friends.

* Who was coming to town, and why did Zacchaeus want to see him?

* Talk about what it's like to be short and not to be able to see what you want to see when there is a crowd of people around you.

* What did Zacchaeus do so he could see Jesus?

* What did Jesus say to Zacchaeus?

* How did Zacchaeus show Jesus that he was sorry about taking too much money from people?

Talk

A TREE

Materials: Brown and green Play-Doh, drawing paper, crayons, and scissors. Optional: an action figure

Make a tree trunk from brown Play-Doh. Then form a ball of green leaves from green Play-Doh to put on top of the trunk. Draw a face, cut it out, and place it to look like Zacchaeus peeking out from the tree. Or put an action figure in the tree. Then use your hands to act out Zacchaeus climbing, walking, and giving back money. Zacchaeus was like a lost person until Jesus found him and saved him so he could be in God's family.

Remember

[I, Jesus,] came to find lost people and save them.

LUKE 19:10

A Thankful Man and Jesus

LUKE 17:11-19

Jesus was on his way to the city of Jerusalem. When he came to a small town, he sat down with one of his disciples.

Way off in the distance, Jesus could see 10 men.
They were walking toward him. As the men came
closer, Jesus saw that they were wrapped up in
scarves and rags. He knew this meant that the men
had a bad skin disease called leprosy.

In Bible times, people with leprosy had to stay
away from healthy people, even their families and
friends. So the 10 men didn't come too close to
Jesus. They didn't want him or any of the people
with him to get sores all over their bodies too.

The men called out, "Jesus, please help us. Please show us that you care about us."

Jesus said to the 10 men, "Go to Jerusalem. And let the priests at God's house see you."

That's not what the men wanted to hear. They thought Jesus would tell them they were well. They thought he would take care of their sores right away. Why did they need to see the priests?

But the men did what Jesus said. They started on their way to see the priests. Then Jesus knew that the men believed him. They trusted him. That pleased Jesus. And he did take their sores away!

The men looked at their hands. They looked at their arms. And they looked at each other's faces. They began smiling. Then they laughed out loud. They were well again!

One of the men ran back to Jesus.

"Praise God! I'm well," he said. "Thank you, Jesus!"

Jesus asked, "Didn't I heal all 10 men? Where are the other nine? Are you the only one who is thankful?"

Then Jesus told the man, "You believed. Now you're well."

Family Time

* Talk together about leprosy in Bible times. There was no medicine for it, and people who had the sores couldn't live at home.

* What did the men ask Jesus to do?

* When Jesus made the men well, how many said thank you? How many forgot?

* All the men believed Jesus made them well, but only one was thankful. Which of the men pleased Jesus?

Talk

ONE THANKFUL PERSON

Materials: 11 wooden clothespins or craft sticks

Make 11 people figures from clothespins or craft sticks by drawing a face on each one. Count nine figures and put them aside. You will have two figures left. One will be Jesus, and the other is the man who was thankful. Use the figures to act out the 10 men coming to ask Jesus for help. They all run off to see the priests. Then they discover they are all well. But only one comes back to say thank you to Jesus. Which of the 10 men do you want to be like?

Always be thankful.
COLOSSIANS 3:15

Bartimaeus and Jesus

MARK 10:46-52

Look at the picture at the top of this page. Do you
see a man sitting beside a road? What else do you
see? A tree? Some bushes? Flowers? The man looks
sad, doesn't he?

The man's name was
Bartimaeus (bar-tih-MAY-us).
He was sad because he couldn't
see anything. He couldn't see
the road or the tree or the bushes.
He couldn't even see the pretty, red flowers.
That's because Bartimaeus was blind.

Bartimaeus couldn't see people, either. But
he could hear them. When he heard people
walking down the road, he would call out, "Hello!
Can you give me a few coins so I can buy a piece
of bread?"

In Bible times there were no jobs for blind people.
So the man had to ask other people for money.

One day Bartimaeus was sitting beside the road near Jericho. He wondered who might be coming down the road that day.

Every day, Bartimaeus sat beside the road. And every day he wished that Jesus would walk by. He knew Jesus was someone very special who could help people.

On this day, Bartimaeus could hear the footsteps of many people. There was such a big crowd that Bartimaeus was afraid they would run into him.

"Be careful," he said. "I need some coins from you. But I don't want to be knocked over."

All of the people were in a hurry. They wanted to be near Jesus so they could hear what he had to say to them.

Bartimaeus was excited when he heard that Jesus was close by. He began to shout, "Jesus, I need your help! I know I don't deserve it. But would you be kind and help me anyway? Please?"

Many of the people in the crowd yelled at Bartimaeus. "Be quiet!" they said.

But Bartimaeus would not be quiet. He shouted louder than before. "Jesus, please be kind to me and help me!"

Jesus heard Bartimaeus calling him. He stopped in the middle of the road and said, "Tell that man to come here."

Someone told Bartimaeus, "Jesus is calling you. He wants you to go to where he is."

So Bartimaeus jumped up. He couldn't see Jesus. But he listened for Jesus' voice. Then Bartimaeus ran toward the voice.

Jesus saw Bartimaeus come. Then Jesus asked, "How would you like me to help you?"

"My teacher," said the man. "I want to see!"

No one but Jesus could help a blind person see. And Jesus did help Bartimaeus. Jesus said, "You trust in me. You believe that I can help you. So now your eyes are well, and you can see."

Right away, Bartimaeus could see. The first person he saw was Jesus! And the first thing he did was to join the crowd of people and follow Jesus down the road. What a happy man he was!

Family Time

Talk

* Talk together about things we would miss seeing if we were blind. Also talk about the way people who are blind get better at using their other senses of hearing, tasting, smelling, and touching.

* How did Bartimaeus know if people were walking down the road?

* Talk about what Jesus said and did when Bartimaeus called to him.

* How did Bartimaeus get to Jesus, and how did Jesus help him?

THE FIVE SENSES

Materials: a scarf for a blindfold; items to see (a stuffed animal or a pillow), hear (a bell or a clock that ticks), touch (a ball or a sponge), taste (an orange or peanut butter), and smell (soap or a flower)

Take turns being blindfolded and guessing what object a family member brings to you. Talk about how God gave each of us eyes, ears, skin, taste buds, and a nose.

Remember

You will call to the Lord, and the Lord will answer you.

ISAIAH 58:9

Jesus and a Ride on a Donkey

MATTHEW 21:1-11; LUKE 19:28-40; JOHN 12:12-15

Jesus and his helpers, the disciples, were on their way to the big city of Jerusalem. But first they came to a small town. The town was on a hillside. Jesus had a job for two of his helpers to do there. Do you see Jesus' helpers? They are waiting to see what Jesus wants them to do.

Jesus told two of the disciples to go into town. What do you suppose Jesus wanted them to find? He wanted them to look for a donkey!

"Go into town," said Jesus. "As soon as you get there, you will see a donkey. It will be a young donkey that no one has ever ridden. And it will be tied to a post."

The disciples wondered why Jesus wanted a young donkey. But they didn't ask any questions. Then Jesus told them, "Untie the donkey and bring it to me. If anyone asks what you are doing, just tell them that I need the donkey."

So the disciples went into town. They found the young donkey, just as Jesus had said they would.

The donkey's owners came over to Jesus' helpers. "What are you doing with our donkey?"

The disciples said, "Jesus needs it." So the owners let the disciples take the donkey.

The disciples brought the donkey to Jesus. They put their coats over it for Jesus to ride on.

Jesus sat down on the donkey. He began riding toward the big city of Jerusalem. Do you see Jesus on the donkey?

There was a big crowd of people near the wall around Jerusalem. They waved branches from palm trees as Jesus rode past them. Can you point to the palm branches you see in the picture?

Some people spread their coats on the road where the donkey would be walking. As Jesus came closer to the city, the people began shouting and singing. They praised God for the wonderful things Jesus had been doing. "Hosanna!" they shouted. "Blessings on Jesus the King. He comes in God's name." What an exciting day!

But there were some leaders who were not happy. They were angry. They didn't love Jesus. And they didn't want him to be their King. Do you see one of the angry leaders in the picture?

These leaders told Jesus to stop the people from praising him. But Jesus said, "If the people keep quiet, the rocks will start talking and praise me!"

Jesus rode into Jerusalem on the little donkey. He waved to the people who welcomed him that Sunday. But Jesus looked sad. Do you have any idea why he felt sad? It was because Jesus knew that the people who welcomed him that day would become his enemies by the end of the week.

Family Time

Talk

* Talk together about Jesus' ride into Jerusalem as a king. What did he ride on? Explain that he rode on a little donkey because he didn't want to act more important than others.

* What were some of the ways the people welcomed Jesus? Talk about parades we have to welcome special people.

* Why were some leaders angry?

* What did Jesus know was going to happen at the end of the week?

A PARADE

Materials: flags and banners (or scissors, felt, and glue to make them), balloons, toy drums, pots, pans, and wooden spoons

Use whatever materials you have for a parade. Pretend Jesus has come to your area and you want him to feel welcome. March around your home, neighborhood, or a park. Sing favorite worship and praise songs as you march. Jesus is our King. We can welcome him every day, because he is with us even though we can't see him.

Remember

**Your king is coming to you. . . .
He is on the colt of a donkey.**

MATTHEW 21:5

Jesus and the Last Supper

**MATTHEW 26:14-16, 20-35; MARK 14:10-11, 17-31;
LUKE 22:1-6, 14-34; JOHN 13:21-38**

One evening, Jesus and his 12 disciples were
getting ready to eat a special meal. It would be
the last supper Jesus would eat with his helpers
for a long, long time. How many of the disciples
can you see?

These are the 12 disciples who were sitting at the table with Jesus: Peter and his brother, Andrew; James and his brother, John; Philip, Bartholomew, and Thomas; Matthew, another James, and Thaddaeus; and Simon the Zealot and Judas Iscariot.

Jesus told his helpers something sad that evening. He said one of them would betray him and give him to his enemies.

Each of the disciples thought,
I couldn't do that! But each one asked
Jesus, "I won't give you to your enemies,
will I?"

Jesus said, "Someone who is eating with me now
will be the one."

As they were eating, Jesus took a loaf of bread
and asked God to bless it. He also took a cup of
wine and asked God to bless that.

Jesus gave Judas some bread dipped in wine.
After Judas ate the bread, Jesus told him, "Hurry.
Do what you planned."

So Judas left. Do you see him? He went to some men who had given him 30 silver coins. He told them where Jesus was. He told them where they could find Jesus later that night.

The other disciples didn't understand where Judas went. They knew he was in charge of their money. So some of Jesus' helpers thought Judas was going to pay for their meals. Others thought he was going to give some money to poor people who didn't have any food.

Jesus told the disciples who were sitting around
the table, "This bread will help you remember my
body. I'm going to give it for you."

Then Jesus told his friends, "I am going to give
my blood for you too. And then God will forgive you
for the bad things you have done. The wine will help
you remember that."

Jesus told his disciples that he would soon have
to leave them. He said, "I have loved you. Now I
want all of you to love one another. If you do, people
will know you are my disciples."

Peter said to Jesus, "If you leave, I'll go with you."

Jesus told Peter, "Before the rooster crows tomorrow morning, you will tell people three times that you don't even know me."

Can you crow like a rooster?

Peter told Jesus he would never say that he didn't know him. But Jesus knew he would. Jesus knew that all his helpers would leave him for a while. But he also knew that all of them except Judas would get together again in three days!

A JESUS FRIENDSHIP BRACELET

Materials: string and yellow, black, red, white, and green beads

You can make a bracelet to show everyone that you always want to be Jesus' friend. Start by tying a knot at one end of the string. Then add the beads.

Yellow: This bead reminds us of heaven, where Jesus is now. It's a bright, beautiful place, and we can live there someday!

Black: This bead reminds us of darkness and the bad things we do. We all do bad things, but Jesus forgives us when we are sorry.

Red: This bead reminds us that Jesus gave his blood for us because he loves us.

White: This bead reminds us that Jesus washes away the bad things we do and makes our hearts clean again.

Green: This bead reminds us that we can grow like grass. We can grow to love Jesus and to know more about him.

Tie the two ends of your string together, and wear your bracelet wherever you go!

Family Time

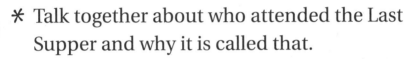

Talk

- Talk together about who attended the Last Supper and why it is called that.

- Which disciple was not a real friend?

- Talk about the bread and the cup of wine. Discuss why the grown-ups in your church take part regularly in a Communion service.

- What did Jesus say about loving one another? What did he tell Peter about a rooster?

Remember

You must love each other as I have loved you.

JOHN 13:34

Jesus in the Garden

**MATTHEW 26:36-50; MARK 14:32-50;
LUKE 22:39-48, 52-53; JOHN 14–17; 18:1-9**

Jesus and his disciples finished their last supper together. Judas had already left. But Jesus talked for a long time with the rest of his helpers. Then he prayed for them and for everyone who would love him someday, including us!

Finally, Jesus said, "It is time." And he took his disciples to a garden with big olive trees.

Jesus said to his helpers, "Sit here while I go and pray." Then he asked his three best friends, Peter, James, and John, to go farther into the garden with him. "Stay here, and watch," he said.

Jesus walked on a little farther. He began to pray to God, his Father in heaven. "Oh, Father," said Jesus. "If it is possible, please don't let soldiers come and take me away tonight. But whatever you want, Father, that's what I want too."

God sent an angel to make Jesus strong.

Then Jesus went back to his disciples. Can you
see what they were doing? They were sleeping!

Jesus said to Peter, "Couldn't you stay awake for
even one hour? You should look around to be sure
that you are safe. And you should pray."

Jesus left his helpers. He prayed to his Father
again. "If you want me to go with the soldiers
tonight, I will do whatever you want."

Jesus went back to his helpers again.
And what do you suppose they were
doing? Yes, they were sleeping again.

Jesus went to pray a third time. He prayed the same prayer again. Then he went back to his disciples.

"Are you still sleeping?" asked Jesus. "It's time for you to get up. A man we all know is coming with some soldiers. And he is going to give me to them."

While Jesus was still talking, Judas came. He had soldiers with him. Judas went over to Jesus. He pretended that he was still Jesus' friend.

"Greetings, Teacher," said Judas. Then he gave Jesus a kiss on his cheek. That's what he had told the soldiers he would do. Then they would know which one was Jesus.

The soldiers grabbed Jesus and arrested him. Jesus asked, "Do you think I am a bad person? Do you think I have done something wrong? I have done nothing wrong. But I will go with you anyway."

Judas was the one who had done something wrong. And the rest of the disciples were afraid. They ran away. Then the soldiers took Jesus away, but only because Jesus let them do it.

Family Time

Talk

* Talk together about Jesus' prayer in the garden. Discuss the fact that Jesus knew soldiers were going to come for him. Also point out that Jesus said he wanted to do whatever his Father wanted.

* Talk about how we can pray the way Jesus did. We can ask God for whatever we want. But then we should add, "I pray that what you want will be done."

* How did Judas let the soldiers know which person was Jesus?

* What did Jesus let the soldiers do?

PRAYER PLAQUE

Materials: white construction paper, a black crayon, bright-colored crayons, and yarn

Use a black crayon to print on three lines: *I pray that/what you want/will be done.* Decorate the plaque with colorful shapes and designs. Hang your plaque where your family can see it and pray the words.

Remember

[Jesus prayed,] "My Father . . . I pray that what you want will be done."

MATTHEW 26:42

Jesus and His Trial

MATTHEW 26:57–27:26; MARK 14:53–15:15;
LUKE 22:54–23:25; JOHN 18:12-40

Soldiers took Jesus away from the garden that night.
They led him to the home of an important priest.
Other teachers and leaders had come to the priest's
house. They were waiting for Jesus.

NO!

Peter followed along behind the soldiers. But he stopped by the gate of the house where they took Jesus. A woman asked Peter, "Aren't you one of Jesus' disciples?"

"No!" he said.

Then Peter came closer to the house. He stood by a fire outside to keep warm. A young woman saw him. She said, "This man was one of Jesus' friends."

NO!

"No!" said Peter.

Later, another person said, "This man must be one of Jesus' disciples."

But again Peter said, "No!" How many times did Peter say no?

NO!

After Peter said three times that he didn't know Jesus, do you know what happened? The rooster crowed, just as Jesus had said it would.

Peter heard the rooster. And then he felt very sad. He left the yard of the house where Jesus was. When Peter left, he was crying hard.

Inside the house, the priest and teachers and other leaders began to ask Jesus questions. They asked, "Are you the Son of God?"

"I am," said Jesus.

Jesus' answer made the priest angry. He said, "No man has the right to call himself the Son of God. What shall we do with him?"

The other leaders said, "He must die!"

The soldiers around Jesus began to make fun of him. They laughed at him, and they even hit him.

Then the Jewish leaders took Jesus to Pilate. Pilate was the Roman governor. And he was in charge of all the Roman soldiers.

A lot of people began to gather. Look at all of them! Pilate asked the people, "What did this man do that was wrong?"

The Jewish leaders made up stories about Jesus. They told Pilate what a bad person Jesus was. Of course, nothing they said was true. Then they told Pilate, "Jesus also tries to make us believe that he is our king."

Pilate asked Jesus, "Are you the king of all these Jewish people?"

Jesus answered, "Yes, it is as you say."

The Jewish leaders kept telling Pilate how bad Jesus was. Pilate said, "Jesus, aren't you going to say something?" But Jesus didn't say a word.

Pilate said, "I find nothing wrong with this man."

Pilate wanted to let Jesus go free. He said, "I'll just have some men beat him up first."

It was the time of year when Pilate always let one person out of jail. It was time to ask the people who that person should be. "Shall I let Jesus be the one to go free this year?"

"No!" the people shouted. "Give us Barabbas." They didn't care that Barabbas had done many bad things. They shouted again, "Barabbas! Give us Barabbas!"

"Then what shall I do with Jesus?" asked Pilate.

"Put him on a cross, and let him die," answered the people. They shouted the same words over and over again.

So Pilate gave in. Soldiers beat Jesus. Then they put a robe on him. And they made a crown from sharp thorns for his head. They made him look like a king, but they didn't treat him like a king. Do you see Jesus' robe? Do you see his crown? The sharp thorns would have hurt Jesus' head, wouldn't they?

Pilate brought Jesus out to the people. He tried one more time to make the people change their minds. But do you see how angry the people look? They wouldn't change their minds.

Pilate said, "I don't want to take the blame for putting Jesus on a cross. That was not my idea."

The people said, "We will take the blame."

But no one knew that Jesus was letting them do this. He was the King, and he was in charge.

Family Time

Talk

* Talk together about the three times when Peter said no. Point out that Peter was probably very scared. He didn't want soldiers to take him away too.

* But Peter should have kept his promise to Jesus. What was it? (See page 387.)

* How did a rooster make Peter feel sad?

* Talk about why the leaders were angry with Jesus. Did they believe that Jesus was God's Son?

* How did Pilate want to help Jesus?

* What did the crowd of people say to do with Barabbas? What did they say to do with Jesus? Jesus knew his job was to die on the cross and take the blame for everyone else's sins. But he also knew he would come back to life.

A CROWN OF THORNS

Materials: aluminum foil, scissors, paper clips, and tape

Cut out a strip of foil three inches wide and long enough to go around your head, plus a couple more inches. Crunch the foil and bring the ends together to make a circle. Overlap the ends and tape them together. Then attach several paper-clip thorns to the top and bottom of the crown. Place it on your head. It's not comfortable, is it? If your crown had real thorns, it would hurt a lot. Jesus deserves a nice crown, because he really is our wonderful King.

Remember

"Tell us, are you the Christ, the Son of God?"
Jesus answered, "Yes, I am."

MATTHEW 26:63-64

Jesus and the Cross

MATTHEW 27:27-50; MARK 15:21-41; LUKE 23:26-49;
JOHN 10:14-18; 19:1-37

Do you remember that soldiers put a king's robe on Jesus? And that they put a crown of sharp thorns on his head? Point to the robe and crown.

Do you see the soldiers laughing? They thought it was funny to make Jesus look like a king. They still didn't know that Jesus is a real king. They didn't know that he is God's own Son!

The soldiers were going to put Jesus on a cross.
They were going to place the cross up on a hill
where everyone could see it.

The cross was made of wood, and it was heavy.
The soldiers told Jesus to carry the cross himself.
But Jesus was tired and weak from the many times
the soldiers hit him.

One of the soldiers found someone to help Jesus carry his cross. The man's name was Simon, and he was from a city in Africa. Do you see a soldier talking to Simon? Where is Jesus?

The soldier said to Simon, "You must carry the cross for Jesus."

Simon did what the soldier said. He picked up the heavy cross and leaned it against his back.

Then Jesus led the way up the hill. Simon followed him with the cross. And the soldiers were walking along with them.

More people came behind them. Many of them were women who were crying. They were so sad about the way Jesus was being treated. But Jesus told the women not to cry for him.

It seemed as if the walk up the hill would never come to an end. But finally, Jesus and Simon and all the others came to the top of the hill.

413

The hill was the place where people who had done bad things were put up on crosses to die.

Jesus had done nothing bad. But he let the soldiers put him on the cross so he could die for everyone else's sins. "Forgive these people," said Jesus to his Father. "They don't know what they are doing."

A sign on Jesus' cross said, "King of the Jews." Some of the leaders laughed. They said, "Jesus helped other people, but he can't help himself."

Jesus' cross was placed in the middle between two other men on crosses. Do you see the three crosses? Which one is Jesus on?

The man on one of the crosses made fun of Jesus. But the other one said, "I know you are really God's Son. Remember me when you go to your Father."

Jesus said, "Today, you will be with me in heaven."

Jesus' mother, Mary, was standing near the cross. She was crying. Do you see her tears? Jesus' disciple, John, was there too. Jesus told his mother, "John will be like a son to you now." Then Jesus told John, "Mary will be like a mother to you. Take care of her."

The sky became darker and darker even though it was the middle of the day. The earth began to shake, and everyone was afraid. Jesus looked up and said, "My God, my God, why have you left me?"

Then Jesus said, "Father, I give my spirit to you." After that, he died. He died because he loves us and wants us to live with him in heaven someday. What a happy day that will be!

Family Time

* Talk together about how Simon helped Jesus with his cross.

* Talk about what Jesus and the men on the other two crosses said.

* Why did Jesus die? Where does he want us to live someday? Jesus came back to life. We'll learn about that in the next story. It's the last one in this Bible.

A CROSS AND SOME SHEEP

Materials: a candle, white paper, watercolors, a brush, a black crayon, cotton balls, and glue

Using the candle as a crayon, draw a cross on white paper. You won't see the cross until you paint the whole paper with watercolors. When the paper dries, sign your name on it with a black crayon. Then glue cotton balls around the cross. We are like sheep, and Jesus is our Shepherd. He gave his life for us so we can live with him in heaven someday.

Remember

I give my life for the sheep.

JOHN 10:15

Jesus and the Empty Tomb

**MATTHEW 27:57–28:10; MARK 15:42–16:20;
LUKE 23:48–24:43; 24:50-53; JOHN 19:38–20:20;
ACTS 1:1-11**

After Jesus died, the people who had come to watch
began to leave. They felt sad. Do you see some of the
people walking away?

But Jesus' friends stayed for a while. There were
both women and men who stayed.

That evening, a man named Joseph asked Pilate for Jesus' body. Pilate said he could have it.

So Joseph took Jesus' body down from the cross. Nicodemus helped him. They wrapped Jesus' body in a long cloth. And they took it to a tomb carved out of rock. The tomb belonged to Joseph.

The men rolled a big stone in front of the opening to the tomb. Then they left.

Pilate sent some soldiers to guard the tomb. He didn't want anyone to come and take Jesus' body away.

Sunday was the third day since Jesus had died. Early in the morning, several women went to Jesus' tomb. They wanted to put good-smelling spices on his body. But they didn't know how they would be able to roll the stone away.

When they came to the tomb, they found a surprise. Do you see the stone? It has been rolled to the side of the opening into the tomb!

Inside the tomb, an angel said, "Jesus is alive! Tell Peter and Jesus' other friends."

One of the women, Mary Magdalene, ran and found Peter and John. "The tomb is empty!" she said.

Peter and John ran to the tomb. John got there first, but he didn't go inside. Peter came and went inside. Then John went inside too. Jesus wasn't there. Was he really alive as he had said he would be?

Mary Magdalene stood outside the tomb. She was crying, because she didn't understand where Jesus' body was. She stooped down and looked inside the tomb again. There she saw two angels.

The angels sat where the body of Jesus had been. One angel sat where Jesus' head had been. The other sat where Jesus' feet had been.

The angels wore white robes. Do you see the angels? Can you count them?

"Why are you crying?" the angels asked.

"Someone has taken the body of my Lord Jesus. I don't know where he is."

Mary turned. She saw someone standing near her. It was Jesus, but Mary thought he was the gardener.

Mary asked the man, "Have you taken Jesus' body away? If you have, please tell me where you put him."

"Mary!" said Jesus.

Then Mary knew who the man was. "Teacher!" said Mary.

Jesus told Mary to find his friends. He said, "Tell them that I am going to God, my Father in heaven."

So Mary found the disciples. "I have seen Jesus," she said. Then she gave them Jesus' message.

It was Sunday evening, and the disciples were eating together in a locked room. They were afraid, because they still did not understand what had happened.

All of a sudden, Jesus was standing in the room with them! "Peace be with you," said Jesus.

The disciples wondered if they should be happy or scared. Was this really Jesus, or were they seeing a ghost?

Jesus asked for some food, so they gave him some fish. When he ate it, the disciples knew that it was Jesus and he was alive.

Forty days after Jesus died, it was time for him to go to heaven. Jesus told his disciples, "Teach people all over the world about me. Remember, I will always be with you."

Then Jesus went up into the sky. He went into a cloud, and his friends couldn't see him anymore.

Two angels came. They said, "Jesus is in heaven now. Someday he will come back in the same way you saw him leave." That's good news!

Family Time

* Talk together about why Pilate wanted soldiers to guard the tomb where Jesus' body was. He wanted to be sure no one took Jesus' body away.

* Talk about what the women found on Easter Sunday morning. Talk about where the stone was, who was in the tomb, and who was not in the tomb.

* Talk about Mary Magdalene at the tomb. Who did she think Jesus was? When did she know he was Jesus?

* Talk about how a piece of fish helped the disciples know Jesus was alive.

* Where did Jesus go forty days after he died? Where is he now? How will he come back to us?

Talk

AN EMPTY TOMB

Materials: a paper plate or bowl, watercolors, a brush, scissors, and tape

Paint the inside of your plate or bowl to look like a cave. Cut the bowl in half. Stand the two halves on the straight edges. With the unpainted side of each half facing out, tape the curved edges together. Cut out an entrance in one side and use it for the stone. Paint some bushes around the entrance. And paint the rest of the tomb and the cut-out piece to look like a rock. Put the rock in front of the entrance. Then peek inside. The tomb is empty, because Jesus is alive!

Remember

I am the living one. I died, but look— I am alive forever and ever!

REVELATION 1:18

Preschoolers and Salvation

Age Four and Younger

As Christian parents and teachers, we sometimes think that we must get our children to receive Christ as soon as they can say the name *Jesus.* We are enthralled by how precious our children's first prayers are, and by how trusting they are of God the Father and God the Son.

It's important to be aware that God's Holy Spirit works in the lives of children just as he does in the lives of adults. When our children are ready to know more about the path to salvation, they will start asking questions. We simply need to be available to listen and answer and move along at each child's pace.

There is no right or wrong age for a child to start learning about the plan of salvation. But most children under the age of five do not understand sin, confession, and repentance well enough to have a born-again experience.

Tell the stories in this book and in other Bible storybooks. Discuss the stories, and let this discussion lead to natural conversations about God's love, Jesus' care as the Good Shepherd, and Jesus' death and resurrection. Keep in mind that there is no need to frighten your child with cliff-hangers. For example, after talking about Jesus' trial and crucifixion, be sure your child knows there is a happy ending.

Age Five and Older

Older preschoolers and their elementary-age siblings can understand who God is and what he has done for them. They can understand the following steps to salvation.

1. We all do bad things that make God sad. If we confess our sins and tell God how sorry we are about our bad thoughts, words, and actions, he will forgive us. He will help us stop doing bad things.

2. God wants us to believe that Jesus is his Son, who died on the cross to take the blame for our sins—the bad things we do. He died and came back to life because he loves us so much.

3. When we tell God that we want to be in his family, he gives us a new life. It's like being born all over again.

4. Satan will still tempt us to do bad things. But Jesus is stronger. He helps us want to do what's right.

5. Someday everyone who is in God's family will live with him and his Son, Jesus, in heaven.

God bless you, your child, and your entire family as you learn to know God better and to love him more each day.

Tape or glue a picture of your family on this page. Remember, everyone who trusts in Jesus also belongs to God's family!